The Bite of the Mango

The Bite of the Mango

by Mariatu Kamara with Susan McClelland

©2008 by Mariatu Kamara and Susan McClelland
Edited by Barbara Pulling
Copyedited by John Sweet
Cover concept and design by David Wyman, wymandesign.ca
Digital image manipulation by Ron Giddings
Interior design by Sheryl Shapiro

Annick Press Ltd.

We acknowledge the support of the Canada Council for the Arts, the Ontario
Arts Council, and the Government of Canada through the Book Publishing
Industry Development Program (BPIDP) for our publishing activities.

ONTARIO ARTS COUNCIL
CONSEIL DES ARTS DE L'ONTARIC

Cataloging in Publication

Kamara, Mariatu
        The bite of the mango / Mariatu Kamara ; with Susan McClelland.

ISBN 978-1-55451-158-7 (pbk.).—ISBN 978-1-55451-159-4 (bound)

        1. Kamara, Mariatu.   2. Sierra Leone—History—Civil War,
1991–2002—Personal narratives—Juvenile literature.   3. Sierra Leone—
History—Civil War, 1991-2002—Children—Biography—Juvenile literature.
4. War victims—Sierra Leone—Biography—Juvenile literature.   5. Amputees—
Sierra Leone—Biography—Juvenile literature.   I. McClelland, Susan   II. Title.

DT516.828.K35A3 2008   j966.404092   C2008-903621-2

Distributed in Canada by: Published in the U.S.A. by:
Firefly Books Ltd.   Annick Press (U.S.) Ltd.
66 Leek Crescent   Distributed in the U.S.A. by:
Richmond Hill, ON   Firefly Books (U.S.) Inc.
L4B 1H1   P.O. Box 1338
                                 Ellicott Station
                                 Buffalo, NY 14205

Printed in Canada.
Annick Press is committed to protecting our natural environment. As part of
our efforts, this book is printed on Enviro paper: it contains 30% post-consumer
recycled fibers, is acid-free, and is processed chlorine-free.

Visit us at: www.annickpress.com

Front cover: child soldier © Nic Bothma/epa/Corbis; hands of African woman
© Getty Images/David Buffington; mango © iStockphoto Inc./Skip O'Donnell; smoke
and sky © iStockphoto Inc./Tadej Zupancic; village in Sierra Leone © iStockphoto
Inc./Icoccia. Back cover: author photo © J.P. Moczulski, Toronto, Canada.

To all the people who were there with me on
this journey, from start to finish.
—Mariatu Kamara

To my grandfather, who taught me to never lie and
to speak my truth fearlessly and "who is my angel."
—Susan McClelland

THANKS/ACKNOWLEDGMENTS

A special thanks to:
Kadi and Abou Nabe, their family, my friends,
and the entire Sierra Leone community.
and
Dr. Beth Hedva
Steve Jarosz and 9 Story Entertainment
Joyce Anne Longfellow
Jeff and Rita Rayman
Carolyn Cavalier Rosenberg in memory of Debbie Cavalier
Sorious Samura and Insight News TV
Greg and Linda Wolfond
The Ontario Arts Council and UNICEF Canada

FOREWORD

In my culture, every story is told with the purpose of either imparting knowledge, repairing a broken bond, or transforming the listener and the teller. Mariatu's story embodies all of these elements. I have been waiting for such a story, one that reminds us all of the strength and resilience of the human spirit.

The Bite of the Mango is a rare account, written in a chillingly honest voice, of how a 12-year-old girl became a victim of one of the most brutal wars of the 20th century. It is the story of how this girl survived to start life over again, after being robbed not only of her childhood but of her hands. She has had to learn to live without them. What does it feel like to be unable to wipe away your own tears of deep sadness, to stand without hands to push you up? Mariatu tells us about these experiences and many more in her narrative of lost innocence, betrayal, and recovery during an arduous and bloodcurdling time. She describes the humility, culture, and interaction of a closely knit village community in Sierra Leone, and explores how war fueled our country's disintegration into a society filled with suspicion and distrust as neighbor turned against neighbor, child against child, and child against parent.

7

This powerful and timely story is told in simple language that captures both the innocence of the teller and her desperation to create a deepening awareness about the suffering of children caught up in the madness of war. "It is difficult to start talking about what happened during the war, but once you start, you have to go on," Mariatu told me when we met in April 2007. I believe that she exemplifies this same strategy in every aspect of her life.

The light and joy in Mariatu's face don't show you that she is someone whose heart once said goodbye to everything she knew. Meeting this remarkable young woman changes one's idea of what it means to be a victim of war. The media often focus on the trauma people suffer, forgetting to tell us about their ability to recover and the humanity that remains intact. Mariatu's story gives that necessary human context to what it means to be both a victim and a survivor, to transform your life and continue to live with vigor.

I am deeply thankful that the world will be able to meet Mariatu through this book.

Ishmael Beah
New York, June 2008

Maps of Africa and Sierra Leone

SIERRA LEONE

Manarma
Magborou
Port Loko
Lunsar
Yonkro

Freetown

Mariatu's route to Freetown

CHAPTER 1

My name is Mariatu, and this is my story. It begins the year I was 11, living with my aunt and uncle and cousins in a small village in Sierra Leone.

I'd lived with my father's sister Marie and her husband, Alie, since I was a baby. I called them Ya for *mother* and Pa for *father*, as terms of endearment. It was common in my country for children in the rural areas to be raised by people other than their birth parents.

Our village of Magborou was small, like most villages in Sierra Leone, with about 200 people living there. There were eight houses in the village, made out of clay, with wood and tin roofs. Several families lived in each house. The adults slept in the smaller rooms, and we kids usually slept together in the living room, which we called the parlor. Everyone chipped in and helped each other out. The women would all cook together. The men would fix the roofs of the houses together. And we kids played together.

None of the kids in my village went to school. My family, like everyone else in Magborou, was very poor. "We need you to help us with the chores on the farm," Marie explained.

Occasionally children from wealthier families and villages would pass through Magborou on their way to and from school. Some of these children went to boarding schools in Sierra Leone's capital city, Freetown. I felt sad when I saw them. I wished I could see for myself what a big city looked like.

Starting from the time I was about seven, and strong enough to carry plastic jugs of water or straw baskets full of corn on my head, I spent my mornings planting and harvesting food on our farm outside Magborou. No one owned land in the villages; we all shared the farm. Every four years or so we rotated the crops of cassava—which is like a potato—peanuts, rice, peppers, and sweet potatoes.

Even though not everybody who lived in Marie and Alie's house was related by blood, we thought of each other as family, calling one another uncle, aunt, and cousin. Mohamed and Ibrahim, two of my cousins, were already living in the village when I arrived as a baby.

Mohamed was about 17—I wasn't entirely sure, since people in the village didn't celebrate birthdays or keep track of how old they were. Mohamed was chubby, with a soft face and warm eyes. He was always trying to make people laugh, even at funerals. Everybody would stay home and mourn when someone in the village died, usually for three days. We didn't work during that time. We sat around, and the adults would cry. But Mohamed would walk in and start making light of everyone's tears.

"If the dead hear you making such a scene," he would say, "they'll come marching back here as ghosts and take over your bodies."

People would look shocked, and Mohamed would then speak more gently. "Really," he would say, "the dead died because it was their time. They wouldn't want you spending your remaining days here on earth crying about them."

Mohamed was a good person. When food was scarce, he'd give his portion to me or the other younger kids, saying, "You eat up, because you're little and need to grow."

Ibrahim couldn't have been more different. He was about a year older than Mohamed, tall and thin. Ibrahim was bossy. When we worked at the farm, he was always telling me and the other smaller kids what to do. If we didn't obey him, he'd kick a shovel or pail or just storm off.

Ibrahim had these episodes in which his body would convulse, his eyes would get glossy, and his mouth would froth. Much later, when I moved to North America, I discovered that the disease he had is called epilepsy.

Magborou was a lively place, with goats and chickens running about and underfoot. In the afternoons I played hide-and-seek with my cousins and friends, including another girl named Mariatu. Mariatu and I were close from the moment we met. We thought having the same name was so funny, and we laughed about lots of other things too. The very first year we were old enough to farm, Mariatu and I pleaded with our families to let us plant our crops beside each other, so that we wouldn't be separated. We spent our nights dancing to the sound of drums and to people singing. At least once a week, the entire village met to watch as people put on performances. When it was my turn to participate, I'd play the devil, dressed up in a fancy red and black costume. After I danced for a while, I'd chase people around and try to scare them, just like the devil does.

I didn't see my parents often, but when I was 10 I went to visit them in Yonkro, the village where they lived. One evening after dinner, as we sat out under the open sky, my dad told me about my life before I went to live with his older sister. The stars and the moon were shining. I could hear the crickets rubbing their long legs together in the bushes, and the aroma of our dinner of hot peppers, rice, and chicken lingered in the air.

"The day you were born was a lucky day," my dad said, sucking on a long pipe filled with tobacco. "You were born in a hospital," he continued, which I knew was very unusual in our village. "Your mother smoked cigarettes, lots of cigarettes, and just before you were about to come out, she got cramps and began to bleed. If you hadn't been in the hospital, where the nurses gave you some medicine to fix your eyes, you would have been blind."

I shivered for a moment, thinking of what life would have been like then.

It was rainy and cold on the day I was born, my dad then told me. "That's a lucky sign," he laughed. "It's good to be married or have a baby on a rainy day."

For a living, my dad hunted for bush meat, which he sold at the market in a nearby town alongside the villagers' harvests. It seemed he wasn't a very good hunter, though, because I knew from Marie that he didn't make much money at it. I knew, too, that he was always getting into trouble, going in and out of jail. The jail was a cage with wooden bars, set in the middle of the village so everyone could peer in at the criminal.

In Sierra Leone, girls spend most of their time with women and other girls, not with their fathers, grandfathers, or uncles. It was nice to be talking with my dad in this way, and I listened carefully as he explained how I had come to be living with Marie and Alie.

My dad had married two women, as many men do in Sierra Leone. Sampa was the older wife; Aminatu, my mother, was the younger one. Before I was born, Sampa had given birth to two boys. Both of them died within a year of coming into the world. When Sampa was pregnant a third time, my dad asked Marie if she would take the child. That way, he hoped the child would live. Santigie, my half-brother, was born three years before me.

Soon after Santigie went to live with Marie, my mom became pregnant with my older sister. Sampa didn't like that. She was a jealous woman who wanted all of my father's attention. So when my sister was born, Sampa sweetly asked my dad to bring Santigie back to live with them.

Marie was my dad's favorite sister. At first, he told me, he didn't want to bring Santigie home, because he knew it would upset her. But eventually he did, as Sampa's sweetness turned sour. She fought with my dad until Santigie moved back in with them. Marie was very sad about it.

Wanting to make both Marie and my dad happy, my mom told Marie that she could raise the child she was expecting. "I don't know whether this child will be a boy or a girl," my mother told her. "But I promise that you can keep the child forever and ever and call him or her your own."

I went to live with Marie as soon as I had been weaned from my mother's milk. For some reason that even my dad forgot, Sampa sent Santigie back to Marie when I was about three. My half-brother and I became very close. We slept side by side on straw mats, ate from the same big plate of food, and washed each other's backs in the river. When we were older, we teased each other endlessly. But three years later, Sampa decided she wanted Santigie back again. He didn't want to go, and I didn't want him to leave either. But Marie and I had to take him back to his mother.

By then, Sampa and my mom were so jealous of each other that they'd have big fights. It was hard to understand what they were arguing about, since they spoke so fast and so loud, but they'd pull each other's hair and spit and kick. When this happened in the house, Santigie and I crept so far back that our spines were flush against the wall. Our eyes would be wide open, staring, and we'd cover our mouths with our hands to stop ourselves from laughing out loud. Two grown women fighting, with their eyes flashing, their bosoms flying, and their dresses pulled up to their waists, was a funny sight. When I saw how Sampa and my mom fought, I was happy that Marie was raising me. I only wished she could raise Santigie too.

A few months after Marie and I returned to Magborou, someone sent word that Santigie was sick. His belly stuck out like a pregnant woman's, we heard. He was so weak he couldn't even get out of bed. The medicine woman gave him all sorts of remedies, but nothing helped. And this time, my dad told me, he didn't have enough money for the hospital. Santigie died at home in the middle of the night.

A strange thing happened to me after Santigie's death. As I was walking one day, I thought I could hear his voice calling me. I turned to look, but there was no one there. This happened several times over the next year. I often wondered in the times that were to come if Santigie was a spirit watching over me.

The evening my dad told me about my early childhood, he stopped talking as some of the village children began to sing and drum in the center of town. This was the evening the townsfolk of Yonkro met to sing and dance, share stories, and gossip, just like we did every week in Magborou.

"Thank you," I whispered to my father.

He nodded his head in response, stood up, and went back into the hut to join the others.

Adamsay was Marie's youngest daughter. She had gone to live with my grandmother when she was very small, and she came back to stay with us when I was about seven and Adamsay was 10. That's when I began to understand a little bit of why my mother and Sampa were so jealous of each other. I got angry when Marie gave Adamsay new clothes or extra food to eat. I would yell at Marie: "She's your own child and you like her better."

My aunt would say: "That's not true!" If I continued to complain, Marie would lose her patience and pull out a tamalangba, or what we called a whipping stick, made from a long, thick weed that grows everywhere. "Don't say such things," she would admonish me, slapping my behind with it. "It's not true."

Despite my jealousy, I liked having a sister. And Adamsay was nice even when I was mean to her. She'd give me extra food sometimes, and she helped me sew up my skirts when I ripped them playing.

The same year I went to visit my parents, I learned that a friend of Alie's wanted to marry me. The man's name was Salieu. He didn't live in our village, but he had relatives who did, so he visited often. One day he walked right up to me while I was playing a game with some other kids. He stood so close I could feel his hot breath on my cheek. "When you grow up, I will be your husband," he announced.

I was scared. When Salieu pulled away, I ran and found Adamsay. "What does this old man want with me?" I asked her.

"Maybe he wants to kiss you," she said, laughing.

"Ugh, how awful."

Adamsay joked around, saying things could be worse. "You could be married off to Abou."

We giggled, thinking of the old widower in Magborou who spent his days sitting in the shade beside his hut, staring at the ground. Adamsay and I made up a game after that. We went through all the men in Magborou and matched them up with all the young girls. I paired Adamsay with the village chairman, who was like the mayor of Magborou, a tall, skinny older man who already had a big family.

A few days after he'd accosted me, Salieu and his parents came to have a chat with Marie and Alie. Adamsay and I were ordered outside to play, even though it was late and we had to get up early to work on the farm the next day. We crouched underneath the window and craned our necks to hear. But we couldn't, because everyone inside was speaking softly.

The next morning, Marie pulled me aside while we were

planting sweet potato and said Salieu wanted me to be his second wife. The marriage would be in a few years, she said matter-of-factly.

"I don't want to marry Salieu," I told Marie.

"But he's my husband's friend, Mariatu," she said, stopping her planting to look at me sternly. "If you don't find anyone else, you will marry him."

Before long, I discovered I *did* have feelings for someone else. Musa was a sweet boy, just a year or two older than me, who lived in a nearby village. From the time we were little, he and I would see each other during planting, since his family shared our farm. He would also come to our village with his family at night to sing and dance.

One afternoon, Musa and I stopped our digging, sat down beside each other, and talked. We gossiped about the other kids. Then we went swimming in the river and splashed each other. Afterwards, we sat alongside the river, dangling our toes in the cool water. This soon became our routine: we'd stop our work early, talk, then swim, and then talk some more. I liked being around Musa. My entire body felt warm.

One day Musa took my hand and said that when we were older, we would get married and have children together.

Afterwards, I told Marie. "Musa's father is a rich man," she snapped. "He's not going to let his son marry a poor girl."

My stomach churned. I held my words inside, for in Sierra Leone children are taught never to disobey their elders. But when I went to sleep that night, I cried. I hid my face as well as I could so Adamsay wouldn't see my tears.

I saw Musa the next day at the farm, and I smiled when he

21

looked at me. "When his father sees how happy we both are, then he'll say yes to our marriage," I told myself. I remembered what my dad had said about me being lucky. "Maybe this will be another time when I am lucky," I thought.

But then the rebels invaded our lives, and everything changed.

It all started during the dry season when I was 11. War had come to Sierra Leone, and our chairman heard that the violent rebels who were destroying villages and killing people in eastern Sierra Leone were headed toward Magborou. The rebels wanted to overthrow the government, which they accused of being corrupt and not helping the people. The rebels were from different tribes across Sierra Leone, including Temne, like us, and I couldn't understand why they wanted to kill poor people or take over our villages, eat all our food and sleep in our houses. But apparently they did.

Whenever we heard a rumor that the rebels were close, the chairman would order all of the villagers in Magborou to flee into the bush. The first time it happened, we abandoned our homes and took nothing with us, hiding in the bush for several days as we listened to our stomachs moan in hunger. After we'd returned safely to the village, Marie and Alie came up with a plan. They filled empty rice bags with dried vegetables and cassava. We all stuffed a change of clothes and some bedding into the bags too. From then on, whenever the chairman said the rebels were on their way again, we would grab our bags and walk into the bush in single file, following Alie.

After a while, the hiding began to seem normal. We would

spread our straw mats in a forest clearing and stay there, sometimes for as long as a month. I wasn't really scared at first. We
kids continued with the games we always played back in the village. We'd sing and call out to each other. Around the fire at
night, we would tell stories or share what we had heard about
the war. We would lie on our backs and stare up at the moon
and stars. I remembered, though, that long ago my father had
told me never to count the stars. "If you do, and you land on the
star that is you, you will die," he said. I wasn't quite sure what he
meant, but I knew I didn't want to die!

As the rumors about the rebels grew more frequent, we
had to keep quieter during our time in the bush. We stopped
cooking our food so the rebels wouldn't see the smoke from
our fires, and sometimes all we ate for an entire day was raw cassava, which is very hard and dry and bland. Everybody talked in
whispers. Chills ran through me whenever I'd hear a noise,
such as a twig breaking in the bush behind the clearing. A few
times I overheard the adults talking. They were saying that the
rebels didn't just kill people, they tortured them. I didn't talk a
lot in the forest after that. When we were in hiding, Ibrahim
would often stay right beside me, making sure I was safe.
During these times, I didn't mind him being bossy.

When reports of the rebels came during the dry season of
the next year, the chairman decided we should all go to
another village, Manarma.

"There are lots of people in Manarma," he told us when we
had gathered to listen to his instructions. "We will be safer there
than here or in the forest."

The day my family left for Manarma seemed to be no

different from any other time we had fled the village. We would go back to our regular lives as soon as the chairman said it was safe to return.

But this time, things would not work out that way.

CHAPTER 2

Palm oil is a vegetable oil that comes from the palm tree. It's deep orange in color, and in Sierra Leone we use it to cook most of our food.

"Whenever you dream of palm oil," my grandmother had told me when I was seven, "blood will spill by the end of the day."

I dreamt a lot about palm oil when I was growing up. And sure enough, whenever I did, I'd cut myself playing tag with my friends or scrape my knee. But on our first night in Manarma, I had my worst dream ever about palm oil. I was standing in a big pit in the ground. It was full of palm oil, which came up to my knees. Beside the pit stood the tin drum we kept full of fresh lake water for the family. The wooden legs that held up the drum were on fire. The water inside was boiling; steam rose from the drum's spouts into the clear blue sky. The wooden legs began to sway and the drum keeled over. As it fell, the drum turned into my head. In the dream, there was no water inside, only palm oil. And as my head fell to the ground, the thick oil coated my body from head to toe.

I woke up screaming. I had been sleeping on the floor on a straw mat beside Adamsay. There were about 15 of us in the room, including the family who owned the hut, Marie and Alie,

Adamsay, Mohamed, and Ibrahim. It was very early in the morning; the sun was just beginning to show through the window on the other side of the room. My scream woke Alie. As he glared at me, I began to shake. I knew he'd be angry at me for making a noise. We'd been told we'd know when the rebels were getting close because we'd hear gunshots; that's why we had to be very quiet. I was afraid Alie would beat me because my scream had been so loud. Alie was a big man. When we kids didn't do what he asked, he liked to show how strong he was by grabbing a tamalangba and beating us hard.

Marie slept soundly beside him as my uncle's piercing brown eyes burned right into me. I worried I was about to get it. Then someone else in the room stirred.

"Try to be quiet," Alie hissed. "You'll get us all killed if you don't." He glared at me again, then laid his head back down on his mat.

I breathed a sigh of relief and wiped the sweat from my brow. The room was already getting hot. I rolled up my mat, smoothed out the cotton dress I slept in, and went outside to see who was awake.

I didn't tell anybody about my bad dream, at least not right away. Once I'd had a look around, I followed a woman I didn't know to the nearby river. After I washed my face, ran some water over my braided short hair, and brushed my teeth with a chewing stick, which was just a twig from a tree, I began helping her wash clothes. I was carrying a plastic jug of water back to the village when Alie approached me. I thought: "No! This is it. I'm in for my beating." Instead, he said he needed me to go and get some food from Magborou.

I wasn't sure I had heard him correctly, so I politely asked, "What is it you want me to do?"

"I want you to go to Magborou with Adamsay, Ibrahim, and Mohamed and get some food from the storage bin," he said.

I was shocked. I stood absolutely still as droplets of water from the jug on my head dripped down my face and back. "What kind of man sends children back to a village that rebels are about to attack?" I thought to myself.

"There are some others going with you," Alie pressed on. "Some men from Manarma. You will be safe with them."

The image from my dream flooded back. I did something children are never supposed to do in Sierra Leone: I looked Alie, an elder, straight in the eyes. I then went further and did something that was almost certain to result in a beating: I spoke back to him. With a confidence I didn't know I had, I replied, "No! I don't want to go." I decided to lie and say I wasn't feeling well.

"You've been washing clothes. I saw you by the river. And now you're fetching water," Alie said. "You're not sick. You go to Magborou and get the food with your cousins."

"I'm not going anywhere today," I insisted. Shaking from head to toe, I told Alie about my dream and my grandmother's prediction. "Something is going to happen today," I said. "It will be bad. If you don't believe me, I will go. But we might never see each other again."

I thought he'd yell at me, but he chuckled. "Just go. I'm sure nothing is going to happen."

I walked back to the house where we'd slept and set the water jug down beside Marie. I began to cry when she too told me I must go. "There's nothing to worry about," she reassured me. "The rebels have never come yet. I'm beginning to think they're not even real. So do what Alie has asked. Go to Magborou."

I was still crying as I left Manarma with Adamsay, Ibrahim, and Mohamed. All I could think about was my dream—the palm oil, the burning water drum—and my grandmother's words: "Whenever you dream of palm oil ... blood will spill by the end of the day."

We never reached Magborou. On the way, we had to pass through another village, and as soon as we entered it, we heard gunshots. A woman in the road said not to worry. According to her, the gunshots were likely from local soldiers, villagers who kept watch day and night for the rebels. "They're just practicing their shooting," the woman explained. But I could tell she was nervous. Her brown eyes were big as saucers, and she spoke in a hushed tone.

About 10 of us had set out for Magborou from Manarma. The older men in our group decided we should wait until the gunfire ended before continuing on. I grew quiet; I was certain something terrible was going to happen. I stood close to Mohamed and watched as a village woman made fu fu, a meal of boiled cassava. The woman invited us to eat some, but I couldn't take more than a few bites. I was too afraid.

When we couldn't hear gunshots anymore, the men announced they wanted to send Adamsay and me back to Manarma. "Just to be safe," said a man I didn't know.

A salesman who went from village to village selling cooking supplies like onions, pepper, fish, and oil came up to me.

He asked me to take some palm oil back to Manarma. I placed the yellow plastic jug on my head, and Adamsay and I set off. I dreaded every step.

When we reached the outskirts of Manarma, we paused underneath a mango tree near the soccer field, our hearts pounding. We couldn't see or hear anybody, which was very unusual, but I tried to explain away the lack of village activity. The chairman of Magborou would put in place a curfew, at any time of the day or night, whenever he felt we were at risk. The curfew meant everyone had to stay indoors.

Then we saw them, coming out of one of the houses— soldiers of some sort, bare-chested, wearing khaki pants, with bullets wrapped around their muscled bodies. Adamsay began to run away. But a man came from nowhere and caught her by the waist. He carried her back and threw her down in the dust beside me. He wore a red bandana around his head and had several guns slung over his shoulders.

I froze. "This is it," I thought. "Today is the day the rumors of the rebels prove to be true."

The soldier ordered me to take the palm oil down from my head. Behind him, I could see why everything was still: the soldiers had taken over the village, and they were going in and out of all the houses, looting them of people's possessions. They tossed most of the items onto a pile in the middle of the road.

Another soldier joined the first one, and the two pushed us into the village, to a spot by the side of a house. They ordered Adamsay and me to sit side by side on the ground. One of the men tied our hands behind our backs with a piece of scratchy rope. "Do you know who we are?" he asked with a toothy grin.

"No," I said. "Are you the soldiers protecting the village?"

I knew they weren't, and that was the wrong answer. He started yelling at me. "There are soldiers here? Where are the soldiers? We are the rebels, and we want to catch these soldiers. Tell us where they are!"

By now, many of the rebels were coming up to us. They poked their faces into ours and then walked away, wearing hideous smiles. Many were speaking to each other in Krio, the most common language in Sierra Leone, which I recognized but did not understand. The rebel who had tied my hands started interrogating me in my language, Temne. "Where do you come from? How old are you?"

Before I could answer, I spied the palm oil salesman. My mouth hung open. I had no idea why he had turned back toward Manarma, since he had been headed to Magborou. The rebel who spoke Temne turned to Adamsay and me and said, "Don't close your eyes."

We watched as the salesman ran down the dirt road, only to be shot in the stomach by a rebel who appeared in front of him. The rebel looked no older than I was. So the chairman had been right, I realized, when he had said some of the rebels were children. I started to cry. I had never seen anyone die before, let alone be killed. But the rebel said he would kill me if I didn't stop crying. "Don't be a baby," he commanded. "I let big girls live."

My cousin started begging him to let her go. Adamsay was always a talker. But I was shocked that even in the face of danger, she kept chattering.

"Just sit and watch everything," the rebel spat, slapping her in the face, forcing her into silence. "If we set you free, we want you to tell other people about what you've seen here."

Then everything began to happen fast. Too fast.

I heard voices coming from the house beside me. The rebels had blockaded the doors and windows with big wooden planks. Inside, one of the rebels told me, were about 20 people. A single voice stood out, that of my friend Mariatu. She was wailing, calling for help, trapped with the others.

My eyes darted away from the house to a terrifying sight. Two rebels were shoving Ibrahim and Mohamed up the road toward us. They were punching the boys in the back to get them to move faster. When my cousins were directly in front of us, the rebels grabbed them by the neck and pushed them down hard into the dirt. Using their gun barrels, the rebels nudged the boys until they were back to back. Then they tied Mohamed and Ibrahim together.

Next, the rebels forced the boys to stare up into the blinding noonday sun.

"Are you the soldiers watching the village?" one rebel yelled at them. "Are you the soldiers? Are you the soldiers?" he shouted over and over again. Mohamed and Ibrahim shook their heads, but the rebel wouldn't relent.

The boys started crying. Ibrahim had wet his pants, and I watched the stain grow. I had to look away when the rebel began waving a knife around their bare backs and scalps.

I tried to find somewhere my eyes could rest, but the first place they landed was back on the house. Three young rebels, no older than me, were walking alongside it, brandishing torches that set the thatched roof on fire. Everyone inside started to scream as the fire became an inferno. A woman with a baby tied on her back managed to punch through the wooden planks blocking one of the windows. The baby had curly black hair and big eyes that were looking all around. One of the young rebels threw down his torch and grabbed the machete slung on his back. In one violent swoop, he chopped off the woman's head. The baby wailed as the woman's body fell back into the house on top of him. Her head rolled onto the road toward me. I started to cry again, and my body convulsed. "Do you want to join them?" the rebel watching over me threatened. Part of me did.

After a while, the screams died down. Silence descended. All was quiet as the smoke from the fire in the house rose to the sky.

Rebels were now streaming out of the bushes, coming to join those who had taken over the village. There were so many—in front of me, beside me, in back of me—that I couldn't count them all. If I had to guess, I'd say there were more than a hundred. Most of the late arrivals were kids. The older rebels shouted orders to the younger ones. The boys would stop and listen, then resume their pillaging of the remaining houses. Straw mats, baskets, rugs, wooden chairs, tables, and clothes were tossed onto the giant pile in the road. The same boys who had burned down the house with Mariatu inside waved their torches along the bottom of the pile, igniting a huge bonfire.

At first I didn't recognize Salieu, the man who had wanted to marry me, as two young rebels pushed him toward an older one for instructions. Salieu's face was bloody, his shirt torn. His hands were tied behind his back. I gasped when he looked over at me. The older rebel shouted something. The two younger ones grabbed hold of Salieu's arms and marched him forward. The rebel who spoke Temne shouted at me, "Do you recognize this man?"

"Y-y-yesss," I stuttered, my eyes glued to Salieu.

"Good," the rebel smiled. "This one is for you. Watch closely!"

The rebels stepped back, then shot Salieu in the head and stomach.

As the younger rebels dragged Salieu's body away, a sound hit me with a jolt. Music. Loud music, but not the African music I was used to. I couldn't understand the words to the songs, and the beat was very different. Some of the men were dancing to the music. Girls not much older than me passed around what looked like cigarettes. As the smoke from the long paper reefers floated toward me, though, I didn't recognize the smell. The girls handed around cups full of palm wine, which the rebel men gulped down quickly, like water. As they drank and smoked, the men's eyes became red and wild, darting back and forth, not really looking at anything. A couple of the men grabbed the girls' waists and kissed them as they passed.

I had never heard of girl rebels before, but there they were. They wore the same combat pants and red bandanas as the boys and men, and a few of the girls carried guns and had bullets wrapped around their bodies in a similar fashion.

"Do you know these people?" the rebel by my side yelled as five boys pushed a woman and a man toward me. The woman and her husband were from Magborou. She was pregnant, days away from giving birth. The man was her husband.

The woman's bare, mud-caked feet scraped along the

ground. Her face was ashen, and black circles lined her eyes. She was obviously exhausted; her body was hunched as if she were about to topple over. The boy rebels propped her up as she held her very large stomach with her hands.

"Don't do this. Don't do this," the man cried out to the boy rebels. "I will give you anything I have. I will go with you and kill whoever you want. Just let my wife live." But the boys ignored his pleas. "We don't take people anymore," one of them screamed at the man. "This is our last attack before Port Loko, so anyone we capture, we kill."

One of the boys pointed his long rifle at the man's back. Two others forced the man into a kneeling position on the ground facing his wife.

In front of us all, and in front of her husband, they killed her and the baby she was carrying.

"Do you like what you have seen?" one rebel asked me.

Marie had told me once about a rumor she had heard. "When the rebels kill, they make the person watching say they enjoyed it, or else that person will be killed too. If you ever get into that position, always say you like what you see, no matter how bad it gets."

So I replied to the rebel, "Yes."

"Good," he spat back. "We may keep you alive after all."

The rebel guarding us grabbed Adamsay by her braids and yanked her into a standing position. He shoved her into the arms of another rebel, who spun her around and dragged her by the hair down the road. I saw her, like a shadow, being pushed into the doorway of a house on the other side of the bonfire.

"Goodbye," my heart said to her. "Goodbye."

CHAPTER 3

I had prayed before, sometimes as often as the five times a day prescribed for Muslims in our holy book, the Quran. The mosque in Magborou was a house made of red clay. At night, kerosene lamps and tiny candles cast the only light. We had a village imam, who conducted the prayers and gave sermons.

Marie had instructed me how to pray for happiness, for a nice man to marry me when I was older, or for a good harvest for that year. The only thing I ever really prayed for, though, was a pretty new dress. Every year for Eid, which marks the end of Ramadan, our fasting season, Marie would present us kids with new clothes that she had bought in Port Loko, a city about half a day's walk away. I loved having a new docket-and-lappa, a two-piece African outfit made from cotton. Prayers worked, that much I knew, for I always did get a new outfit for Eid.

After Adamsay disappeared into the house with the rebels, I closed my eyes and began to pray and pray and pray. This time, it wasn't for new clothes. "Please let me die quickly. Let it be over quickly. Let my family, if they have been captured by the rebels all die quickly, too. Don't let the rebels cut my body piece by piece."

I prayed hard, so hard my head began to throb. When I

opened my eyes, there was a group of rebel boys staring right at me. If it hadn't been for their red eyes, their guns, and the knives in their hands, it would have been like opening my eyes after counting to a hundred during a game of hide-and-seek, and finding the village kids smiling in front of me.

I felt dizzy. My eyes wouldn't focus. I stopped hearing things, and then my vision went too. I passed out.

When I came to, the first thing that struck me was the music. It pounded in my head. The men and boys were singing along to it, some even screaming lyrics that I couldn't understand. Above the singing, the rebels were yelling some words to each other that I recognized only later, when I moved to North America. *Rambo. Red Eye. Killer.*

I had to pry my eyes open; they were caked shut from my tears mixing with the dirt and dust. At first, all I could see were red and yellow shadows. I could feel heat on my body, like the hot sun in the middle of the day. But as my focus sharpened, I realized that the shadows and the heat were from the bonfire of the villagers' possessions. It was raging now, so big I couldn't see the village anymore. The men and boys danced before it in silhouette.

I was lying on the road where I'd fallen. My hands were now untied, but they were numb from having been shackled by the rope for so many hours. I still managed somehow to gather fistfuls of the dry red earth, which I rubbed into my hair, face, shoulders, and legs. "If I am dirty, the rebels won't want anything to do with me," I told myself.

"Take her to the river to clean up," the man who spoke

Temne bellowed. I hadn't seen him, but he was there behind me, as he had been from the beginning. He barked his order to four boy rebels.

"Wait," I pleaded as the older rebel pulled me to my feet. "I have to pee! Please, can I go pee before you kill me?"

The man let go of me and stepped back. "But we're not going to kill you," he said with a small smile. "We're going to take you with us. You're pretty. There are things you can do for us."

"But I thought you said you weren't capturing anyone else."

"I lied," said the man.

I don't know where it came from, but I had had a feeling earlier that this rebel wanted me to go with him into the bush and to raid other towns. When I first saw rebel girls doing the cooking, I momentarily pictured myself frying cassava alongside them.

"Okay," I replied. All I could think of was to play along with the plan. "I will go with you. But let me pee first."

The man stood back and motioned for the boy rebels to come forward. "Watch her," the man told them. "Don't let this little one run away. I like her." He ran his right hand along my cheek, and as he stepped away he winked. I shuddered.

The rebel boys let me go inside the outhouse alone. I was surprised and grateful for the solitude. I sank to the ground and cupped my face in my hands. I didn't know what to do. I could try to escape by making a dash for the bushes, but I'd have to run through the open soccer field first. I remembered the smirking faces of the boy rebels after they had killed the pregnant woman. The boys standing outside the outhouse would wear the same smirks, I felt sure, after using me for target practice.

"So I will go with them," I decided in a panic. But I didn't want to be one of those girls. My body began to shake. A knot formed in my throat. Choking back tears, I straightened my back and slapped my cheeks. "Pull yourself together," I admonished myself. "You will outsmart them. Go with them. Act as if you like them and would never run away ... and then run away when you have your chance."

Thoughts of Adamsay, Ibrahim, Mohamed, Marie, and even Alie flooded into my mind. They stood in front of me, smiling. I said goodbye to them all.

"Please help me, Allah," I prayed again. "Let me find a way to escape."

The rebel boys had started shouting. "What is taking you so long?" one demanded in Temne.

I didn't bother to answer. I came out a few seconds later, turned, and walked back to the man giving the orders, with the boys trailing me.

The older rebel stood talking to another man, someone I had not noticed before.

The second man had very light skin, almost white. The two were speaking Krio. Their arms were flailing, they were shaking their heads, and their faces were red with fury. As soon as they saw me, they pointed my way. "They're angry about me," I thought.

I knelt down in front of my captors, lowered my head, and waited. I wanted to show the older rebel that I would be obedient.

"Okay, little one," said the rebel as the second man walked away. "Get lost. We don't want you after all."

I wasn't sure I had heard the words correctly, so I remained still.

"You can go," the man repeated, waving his hand this time. "Go, go, go!"

I stood up slowly and turned my body toward the soccer field.

"Wait!" the rebel hollered. I stood motionless as a couple of the boys grabbed guns from their backs and pointed them at me. I waited for the older rebel's order to shoot. Instead, he walked in front of me. "You must choose a punishment before you leave," he said.

"Like what?" I mumbled. Tears I could no longer hold back streamed down my face.

"Which hand do you want to lose first?"

The knot in my throat gave way to a scream. "No," I yelled. I set off at a run for the soccer field, but it was no use. The older rebel caught me, his big arm wrapping around my belly. He dragged me back to the boy rebels and threw me to the ground in front of them.

Three boys hauled me up by the arms. I was kicking now, screaming, and trying to hit. But though they were little boys, I was tired and weak. They overpowered me. They led me behind the outhouse and stopped in front of a big rock.

Gunfire filled the night. The rebels were shooting up the village, I assumed, and probably everyone left in it. "Allah, please let one of the bullets stray and hit me in the heart so I may die," I prayed. I gave up the fight, and I surrendered my fate to the boys.

Beside the boulder, a shirtless man lay dead. Smaller rocks

lay all around him. With a shock, I realized it was the pregnant woman's husband. He traded goods from town to town, like the man who had given me the palm oil. The woman who had been killed was his second wife, and the baby would have been his first child. Now the man's face was nothing but a bloody pulp. I could even see parts of his brain. The rebels had stoned him to death.

"Please, please, please don't do this to me," I begged one of the boys. "I am the same age as you. You speak Temne. So you might be from around here. We would have been cousins, had we lived in the same village. Maybe we can be friends."

"We're not friends," the boy scowled, pulling out his machete. "And we're certainly not cousins."

"I like you," I implored, trying to get on his good side. "Why do you want to hurt someone who likes you?"

"Because I don't want you to vote," he said. One of the boys grabbed my right arm, and another stretched my hand over the flat part of the boulder.

"If you are going to chop off my hands, please just kill me," I begged them.

"We're not going to kill you," one boy replied. "We want you to go to the president and show him what we did to you. You won't be able to vote for him now. Ask the president to give you new hands."

Two boys steadied me as my body began to sway. As the machete came down, things went silent. I closed my eyes tightly, but then they popped open and I saw everything. It took the boy two attempts to cut off my right hand. The first swipe didn't get through the bones, which I saw sticking out in all different shapes and sizes. He brought the machete down again in a different spot, higher up on my arm. This time, my hand flew from the rock onto the ground. The nerves kept it alive for a few seconds, and it leapt from side to side, as trout did when we caught them from the river, before we knocked them on the head and killed them to cook for our evening meal.

I had no energy left as a boy took my other arm and held it down on the boulder. It took three attempts to cut off my left hand. Even at that, some of the flesh remained and hung precariously loose.

I didn't feel any pain. Maybe that was because my hands were still numb from having been tied together for so long. But my legs gave way. I sank to the ground as the boy wiped the blood off the machete and walked away.

As my eyelids closed, I saw the rebel boys giving each other high-fives. I could hear them laughing. As my mind went dark, I remember asking myself: "What is a president?"

CHAPTER 4

My head seemed to be made of cement. My eyes opened, but before they could focus I began to cough. As I raised my right arm to cover my mouth, I could feel blood, warm and sticky. Horror gripped my body, and I remembered: *I have no hands.* Before fear could overtake me, I felt a surging pain in my stomach. My injured arms instinctively cradled my abdomen. "What happened to me?" I said out loud. No one answered.

Standing was difficult without my hands to push me up. I rolled around in the earth, onto my knees, and staggered to my feet. At first I walked around in a circle. I didn't know which way to go. Then I regained my senses. I could hear the loud crackling of the bonfire, and its light shone through the trees, illuminating my way.

Still holding my abdomen, I started to put one foot in front of the other. I wanted to get away … away from here, away from this village. I was certain, though, that I was being set up. Some boy rebel was hiding behind a mango tree, waiting to shoot me. As I walked toward the soccer field and the bushes that lay beyond it, I was waiting at the same time for the sound of a bullet ripping through the air.

42

But the bullet never came, and my walk turned into a run. Soon I could no longer hear the loud music, the roaring flames, or the rebels' cries and cheers. The soft calls of crickets welcomed me into the bush.

I was very weak, but I didn't stop running until I was well into the bush and had reached a pond lit by the rays of the full moon. I knelt down at the edge. My arms tucked into my stomach, I placed my face right in the water. I drank for a long time. The liquid was cool and refreshing.

Afterwards, I sat up and looked down at myself. My docket-and-lappa was torn, dirty, and bloody. I pushed my arms out to examine my wounds. A thick layer of drying blood was all that remained where my hands used to be. I realized suddenly that I was in pain—sharp, darting pain that ran up and down my arms as well as through my abdomen. I was sick, sicker than I'd ever been in my life, that much I knew for certain. I closed my eyes so that I didn't have to look at my wounds, then dipped my forearms into the water, thinking the action would soothe my injuries. It didn't. The pain was overwhelming. Its intensity made me dizzy, and I felt myself fainting.

"Don't pass out," I repeated to myself as I lay on the grass. I forced my eyes to remain open as I took a few deep, long breaths. I thought of my family, of my mother and father. Were they alive? Had the rebels reached them? And then I thought about my life. I heard a voice in my head. "You will live," it said. "You will live."

When my breathing had returned to normal and my head no longer spun, I sat up and looked around. Baskets of laundry and clothes were littered everywhere. "Villagers never abandon their laundry like this," I thought. "They must have been spooked, perhaps by the sound of the rebels' gunfire." I stood up slowly, and awkwardly approached one of the wicker baskets. Using my right foot, I rummaged through it. The clothes inside were still damp from the washing, but I didn't care. I pulled out what appeared in the moonlight to be a blue lappa, a garment like a sarong. I tried to wrap the fabric around my torso, but without my hands I couldn't do it. The lappa fell between my arms onto the ground.

I straightened my back and picked the fabric up again between my toes. This time I wrapped the lappa around my injured arms. As soon as I could find a path, I resumed my run through the bush.

The Sierra Leone countryside is crisscrossed with paths that villagers use to travel from their homes to the farms, to the ponds for washing, and to other villages. This path, I felt, was leading me away from Manarma. But where I was going, I didn't know.

After a while I slowed my pace to a steady walk and began shouting: "Ya Marie! Pa Alie! It's me, Mariatu!" I hoped that my aunt and uncle had escaped the rebels and were hiding in the darkened forest of coconut, avocado, and mango trees. "Help!" I called out. But the only response was from the crickets and owls that stopped their songs as I drew near.

Eventually the path led me to an abandoned farmhouse.

I could see that the farm had not been tilled in at least one season, maybe more.

It was overgrown with weeds and tall grasses swaying in the gentle wind of the night. A farm was a good sign. It meant that a village was nearby—and help. But relief soon gave way to terror. What if the rebels reached the village before me? I took a few more deep breaths, then made myself enter the farmhouse.

Moonlight shone through a gaping hole in the thatched roof. There was a bench along one wall, and I let my body sink down onto the wood. As I closed my eyes, I blocked out any other thoughts by repeating to myself: "I'm alive. I will stay alive."

I don't know if I actually slept or not. But a hissing noise jarred me wide awake. I lifted my head with a jolt and saw beside me a jet-black cobra. Its long body was coiled on the floor just below the bench, and its big head, with its spitting pink tongue, was reaching up toward me.

I slowly rose from the bench and backed away. From the doorway, I saw the snake pulling its head back down into its body. I was puzzled. "Why didn't you want to hurt me?" I asked the creature. "Is it that you sensed my pain?" The cobra looked at me for a moment while I stood paralyzed with fear and curiosity. Eventually, the snake turned its head away.

I ran and ran once I reached the path again. As soon as I started calling out for Marie and Alie, though, I spied another cobra, this one spanning the width of the path before me.

I stopped dead in my tracks. My grandmother had once told me that every person has a spirit watching over him or her. Some people, if they're really good, have two or three spirits. These spirits are often relatives who have died, like a grandfather, like Santigie, and sometimes they come to you in the guise of an animal, a bird or a reptile. Here I was looking at the second black cobra of the night. Something was going on, that much I was sure of.

"What are you doing?" I yelled at the snake. I felt very frustrated, for I wanted to get on my way and couldn't—the cobra was blocking the path. "If you are the spirit of my guardian angel, please get out of the way to let me pass." The snake didn't move.

With a determination I didn't know I had, I plunged into the dark bush. The moonlight couldn't penetrate the canopy formed by the trees, so I tripped over rocks and long, twisty weeds. But every time I lost my footing, I got right back up. I worked my way around in a semicircle, coming out on the path far beyond where I'd seen the snake.

I walked until the sun began to rise, casting long shadows in front of me. I tried to push on steadily, in the hope that I would arrive at a village the rebels had not yet reached. But every now and then I'd jump at a sound. The cooing of an owl or the snap of a twig caused by some small animal made me think the worst—that the rebels were there in the bush around me, taunting me, letting me believe I was safe only to kill me at a later time. I knew my mind was trying to get the better of me. "There are no more cobras. There are no rebels," I chastised myself.

Finally, up ahead, I saw a clearing, and the waves of a small lake. I quickened my pace. I was thirsty by now, and hungry too. I thought, "When I reach the lake, I will drink and try to eat some fruit from one of the trees." I also thought I would unravel the fabric to see what my arms looked like. But as I neared the clearing, two dogs, one jet-black and the other one brown and white, leapt out at me from the bush. The black dog was barking like I had never heard a dog bark before. Its body kept lunging forward, as if it wanted to jump on me, and saliva frothed from its mouth.

Every village had many dogs. Nobody claimed them as pets. Instead, everybody fed them, and all the kids played with the puppies. Dogs weren't allowed in the houses. The women would shoo them away when they tried to enter. But they would walk with us to the farm and follow us kids whenever we played games. Tiger, a tawny brown mutt, was my favorite in Magborou, although he drove me crazy by always nipping at my ankles.

Dogs wouldn't be so deep in the bush alone; there had to be people somewhere near. But I was too frightened of the black dog to continue along the path. I didn't want to go back the way I had come, though, for that path led back toward the rebels. Ever so slowly, I crept into the bush again and tiptoed deep into the trees.

Growing up, I'd heard stories of little kids who'd wandered too far into the bush and got lost. Their families never saw them again. "A big fat boar must have eaten them," Alie would say. I remembered his words now, as I walked through the forest. What if, after all I had been through, I were to get eaten by a huge wild boar?

Before too long, I found another path. I followed it until I reached a crossroad. That's when I saw him, the first person since Manarma. A man, tall and slender, was coming along one of the other paths. He stopped when I called out "Hello." He looked me straight in the eye, and his jaw dropped. I sensed his fear even before he spun around and ran away from me. I didn't think twice: I followed him. His legs were longer than mine, and the rebels hadn't injured him as far as I could see, so I quickly fell behind. But I pushed on. I was determined to catch this man.

47

The path ended at a village. When I came out into the clearing, I could see the man leaning against a hut, trying to catch his breath. I too stopped running. The man gaped at me. I walked slowly toward him, noticing that all the buildings in the village were covered in the long, twisted branches of mango trees. As with the farmhouse where I had met the cobra, the inhabitants had long since abandoned this town.

"What do you want?" the man questioned me as I neared.

"I am very sick, and I need your help."

"What happened to you?" he asked.

I opened my mouth to answer, but nothing came out. I tried again. Still nothing. "I'm hungry," I finally managed to whisper.

The man bent down and picked up a mango. He passed it to me, and when I didn't raise my arms to receive the fruit, he looked down and saw the bloodied fabric.

"They cut off your hands!" he burst out angrily. "Those bastard rebels! I knew you were hurt. That's why I ran—I thought they might be nearby with you. You need to go to the doctor. But I can't take you there. The rebels shot my wife's mother in the leg. I have to find someone to help me carry her to Port Loko, for she can't walk. I can't help both of you. Here," he said, holding the mango up to my mouth for me to eat. But I shook my head. I couldn't eat from his hands. It felt wrong to be fed like a baby.

"Put it in there," he said, lifting my arms gently and placing the mango in between the folds of the fabric. I raised my arms and managed to take a few bites of the juicy fruit. As I ate, the man explained that he was from Manarma. He and his family

48

had fled into the bush when they heard the rebels approaching. His wife's mother was an old woman who couldn't run fast enough, and so she was shot.

"I don't remember seeing you at the village," he said afterwards. "But then, I don't really know what you look like. You are covered from head to toe in dirt and blood."

I just stared at the man, whose name I never asked. Finally, my tears began to flow. "I want to go home," I sobbed. "I want to go home." I said it over and over again.

The man took me by the shoulders. "You need to go to a hospital," he said. "You will die before you make it back home if you don't. There's a clinic in Port Loko, which is not far from here. I'll tell you what I will do: I will walk you to the road that goes to Port Loko, and I will leave you there to find your own way."

"The rebels said they were going to Port Loko next," I choked out between sobs. "I can't go there ... not alone."

"You will be fine," the man replied in a soothing voice. "There are government soldiers in Port Loko. It's safe, even if the rebels try to attack. It's the *only* place to go, my sweet child. Without the medicine you can get in Port Loko, you will die."

He was right. I knew that. I had to try. I wiped my tears away with my arms and motioned with my head for the man to lead on. I followed closely behind as he assumed a steady pace back along the path we had just traveled. We didn't stop, nor did we say a word to each other, until we reached the road to Port Loko.

The road was lined with thick elephant grass, shrubs, and different kinds of fruit trees. That frightened me, for rebels could easily hide in these bushes. I looked deep into the man's eyes. "Please take me with you," I pleaded. "Please! I don't want to die."

He placed one hand tenderly on my cheek. With his other hand, he cupped my chin. "You will die if you come with me," he said in a soft voice. "I don't think you know how sick you are. But I do. Follow the road, and by midday you will find yourself in a village only a short distance from Port Loko. Someone there will take you the rest of the way, I am sure."

Before he left, the man wiped my face with a dirty blue rag.

"I'm scared," I whispered.

"I know," he said. "We're all scared. But you have to go. Goodbye."

I watched as he ran back down the path, leaving me standing in the middle of the dusty red clay road all alone.

CHAPTER 5

In Magborou, we kids played with stilts made from slabs of wood, tin cans, and rope. In addition to seeing who could walk the fastest on them, we'd try to knock each other down. Usually there were too many kids for the number of stilts, so we'd end up sharing. My friend Mariatu would stand barefoot on my feet and hang on to me, usually around the neck. I would hold on to the ropes. Walking was hard with four feet, even though Mariatu tried to lift her own feet in rhythm with mine. With her on top of me, it felt as if I weighed twice as much, and we'd always end up laughing and falling on top of each other.

That's how I felt as I began the long walk into Port Loko— as if my body weight had doubled. But now Mariatu was gone, and I was terrified. My arms throbbed, particularly near the bottom, around my wounds.

There wasn't a cloud in the sky, since it was the dry season. The sun was hot already, even though it was still morning. The air was heavy with the smells of the forest—decaying wood, mango blossoms, and dew—and dust from the road. Birds cawed and chirped. I startled in fright the first few times I heard

51

the birds. In my imagination I saw rebels camouflaged in their khaki pants, sneaking through the bushes beside me. With every step I could hear the order from the older rebel to the kids in his charge: "Shoot that girl!"

By noon, my bare feet were covered in blisters. I trudged on, telling myself that the village the man mentioned must be near.

Sure enough, not long after, the lush countryside opened up. As the trees became more scarce, I heard the first sounds of a village—children's laughter and the rustle of leaves.

I quickened my pace until I was in the center of the village. I could still hear the children, but the village was much quieter than it normally would have been. Two women with their backs to me were making what looked like fu fu and rice in large steel pots. Another woman sat by their side, mending a pair of boy's pants.

"Hello," I said as loudly as I could. My voice came out like a whisper, since my throat was parched. None of the women heard me. But someone else did.

"Who are you?" a young boy called out. Bug-eyed, he pointed a long finger at me, the way the boy rebels had done with their weapons.

The women jumped up, dropping whatever they had in their hands.

"What do you want?" demanded one of them. She appeared to be the oldest of the three, with wisps of gray in her short hair. She took a few steps toward me, then stopped. "What do you want?" she repeated. She looked very stern.

"P-p-please," I stammered, my voice now a little louder.

"I need help." I felt my legs wanting to collapse, but I managed to stay upright. "Rebels—"

"Rebels send girls like you into the villages first," the woman cut in. "Then, when we're caring for your needs, they attack. Where are they?" She was a heavy woman, and her sturdy legs shook the ground as she stamped. "Tell me where they are, child! Where are the rebels?"

"There are no rebels," I said weakly. The woman's temples were throbbing, and sweat trickled down her neck onto her bare breasts. "Please," I begged. "I'm hurt." And with that, I fell forward into the woman's arms.

The woman who had caught me laid me down on the dusty ground. The sewing woman was taller, with a narrow face and high cheekbones. She propped the pants she had been mending under my head as a pillow while the third woman ran off, calling for help. The oldest woman lifted a plastic cup full of water to my lips. I sipped at it. I dared not drink too much, since my abdomen was starting to hurt again and I was afraid I would throw up.

The woman holding the cup explained that she had heard of girls like me being used as decoys. My mind drifted back to the girls I'd seen in Manarma with the rebels. Apparently the girls would feign injury and get unsuspecting villagers to help them. While everyone was busy with that, the rebels would sneak into the village unnoticed and attack.

The two women washed my face and then delicately unwound the fabric around my arms.

"Your wounds are very serious," the older one said. "We need to get you to the medical clinic in Port Loko. Can you walk?"

I nodded, and the two women helped me stand. They walked beside me, close enough to catch me if I fell. We made our way back to the main road and started our trek into Port Loko.

After a while the road filled with women carrying big basins of fruits and vegetables on their heads. I looked down to avoid their stares, but I could feel them looking at me.

Then a voice called out: "You. You. You!" When I looked up, a bare-chested man was pointing at me.

The two women stopped and told me to do the same.

"You!" the man continued, coming right up to me. "Look at this person," he demanded. He pointed at a man being dragged toward us. The captive had a rope around his neck and his wrists tied behind him, like Adamsay's and mine had been in Manarma. "Do you recognize him?" the bare-chested man barked.

I did recognize the man who was tied up. He had married a beautiful woman from Magborou not long before. When he first announced his intentions to the people of our village, he and his family were given big cups full of water, as a symbol of approval, peace, and purity. The entire village turned out a month later to watch the man arrive for the week-long wedding ceremony. He came laden with food. The woman's family had sent, via messenger, a list of what they wanted: a goat, a big bag of rice, beans, fried dumplings, and fruit. As is customary in our culture, the man had presented his bride-to-be with a calabash, or gourd, full of household items, including a needle and thread, candies, and a copy of the Quran. Also inside was a dowry of several thousand leones, the money we used in Sierra Leone, which the bride's family distributed among her relatives.

For the ceremony, the woman wore a lovely white docket-and-lappa with lace sewn into it and a matching head scarf. The man was dressed in a gold and brown gown and cap. I didn't know him, but he seemed nice, taking my hand at one point during the festivities and dancing with me. Now here he was, being dragged down the road like the wedding goat being led to slaughter.

I hesitated, not sure what to do. "Yes, I know this man," I finally said to the fellow standing in front of me. "He's—"

But the man cut me off. "I thought so," he said angrily. "We caught him with an army sack and a red bandana like the rebels wear. He is one of the rebels. Even if he didn't personally cut your hands off, we will kill him in your honor."

"No, wait!" My voice was thin and scratchy. "I know him from my village." My head was spinning, and I was so weak I was certain I would collapse any minute. I tried so hard to get the words out to tell the man to stop. But I couldn't.

By now, all the people in the road had moved to the sides as spectators. The man who had accosted me pointed his long gun at the captive.

Bang. Bang. Bang. The three gunshots echoed in my head as the man I knew from the wedding fell backwards onto the ground.

I closed my eyes.

"No more," I prayed to Allah. "No more bloodshed!"

The hospital clinic in Port Loko was a square building made of gray cement. People of all shapes and sizes were waiting for help—old men, women holding screaming and bloodied babies, young children cradling their arms like me.

The two women led me to a vacant spot under a mango tree. I tried to prop myself up against the tree trunk, but I couldn't manage it. I slumped to the ground and entered a fitful sleep, in which I kept seeing people being shot.

At some point, the older woman shook me awake and helped me sit up. "Come," she said, guiding me. "The nurses can see you now."

Inside the clinic, it was even hotter than outside. A wind ruffled the dirty white curtains that hung over the windows, but there were so many people lying on the bare floors and leaning up against the walls that the breeze didn't get very far. I found it hard to breathe.

A woman wearing a stiff white dress and matching cap took me by the shoulders. She was a nurse, she explained, and she would help me as best she could. After I lay down on a metal bed, she put a thin blanket the color of the sky over me.

I closed my eyes and drifted, but I was aware of everything going on around me: women speaking softly, children whimpering. Occasionally someone screamed, and when I heard that, my body twitched. "We want to go to Port Loko next," the rebels said inside my head over and over again.

I felt the nurse unwind the fabric from my arms. "Where did this happen to you?" she asked.

"Manarma," I groaned.

"Who did this to you?"

"The rebels." As I said the words, I panicked. "They said they're coming to Port Loko next," I repeated hysterically, trying to sit up.

The nurse attempted to calm me. "You are safe here. ECO-MOG[1] patrols the city. Even if the rebels attack, they will be killed."

"You don't know what they are capable of doing," I insisted, shaking my head from side to side.

"There is an ECOMOG truck here taking the sickest people to Connaught Hospital in Freetown," the nurse continued. "We don't have the medications here to fight your infection. You must go with them."

As she helped me sit up, I noticed for the first time that the nurse was pretty, with high cheekbones and smooth black hair brushed neatly underneath her cap. She looked only a few years older than me.

I felt dizzier than ever. My stomach convulsed. I started to vomit, but nothing came out. The nurse supported me as I got back on my feet, then led me down a crowded hall to the back door of the clinic. As soon as she opened the door, I began to scream. She grabbed hold of me as I tried to run away.

"Rebels!" I shouted. "Rebels!"

"No," the nurse said in a reassuring voice. "These men are with ECOMOG. They're here to help you. They're on your side."

I looked more closely at the three men standing by the truck. They wore the same khaki pants as the rebels, and guns and bullets were draped around their bodies too. The only thing different about them was their matching khaki shirts and hats.

1 ECOMOG stands for the Economic Community of West African States Monitoring Group. It was a military operation deployed in Sierra Leone to help end the war.

One of the soldiers smiled at me. "May I touch you?" he asked, stepping toward me.

I said nothing as he lifted me onto the back of the truck. There were benches lining the sides, and a green tarp covered the top. The rest was wide open.

A soldier inside found me an empty place to sit. As I glanced around at the bloodied faces of the others, I shivered. There were people with no ears, some with no arms, and one person with an eye missing.

Then my heart stopped. I gasped as I looked into the sad brown eyes of first Mohamed and then Ibrahim.

CHAPTER 6

One afternoon when I was little, I was sitting underneath a coconut tree when a tiny yellow and brown weaver dropped suddenly from the sky. I don't know what made that little bird fall, but it landed with a thud on the red clay earth. I moved to help it, then decided not to. The weaver was injured. It was better off dying on its own than having me take it back to the village, where it would likely die in pain a day or two later or, worse, live out its life with a broken wing. For the longest time, I watched as that stubborn bird tried to stand up on its crooked little legs, flapping its wings wildly, only to topple over and lie still before trying all over again.

Then something miraculous happened. After the bird had lain motionless for so long I thought it was dead, it stood up as solid as ever and lifted off into the sky.

When I saw Ibrahim and Mohamed, I felt like that bird. Something had knocked me clear out of the sky, and here I was on the ground, trying to get up. But I couldn't, and I wondered if I'd ever have the perseverance of that small weaver. I sat in a trance, not moving. My glazed eyes locked on Ibrahim's eyes, then moved to Mohamed's. What broke the spell was Ibrahim.

With a defeated sigh, he looked down at his arms, which were bandaged like mine. "The rebels cut off his hands too." I gasped at the realization. And then I saw that Mohamed was cradling his arms in exactly the same way.

I felt a chill, though it was very warm in the back of the truck with all our bodies crammed so close together. My head slipped onto the shoulder of the person sitting next to me.

"I'm sorry," I said.

"Don't," a soft female voice replied. The woman gently pushed my head back down onto her fleshy shoulder, then stroked my forehead with her fingers.

To avoid the rebels, the ECOMOG truck took a longer route to Freetown, along a rough road full of potholes and ditches. Somehow I managed to catch a bit of sleep, with my head still on my neighbor's shoulder.

I woke when the truck stopped, and the woman turned toward me.

"What happened to you, sweet girl?" she asked quietly, wiping some hair out of my eyes. "No. Don't answer. Save your voice."

She poured some water onto a cloth, then ran it over my forehead and cheeks. "My name is Fatmata," she said. "My uncle was caught in the attack at Manarma, like you, I am guessing. My brother and I are here with him." She gestured to the two men sitting beside her. One of them was covered from head to toe in caked blood.

ECOMOG soldiers were helping people disembark from the truck. My body tightened when it was my turn, and my lips started to quiver. Fatmata sensed my anxiety. "We're in Lungi," she told me. "We need to take a boat to Freetown, just a short distance over the water."

It was dark by now, and on the far shore I could see lights going up the sides of buildings taller than palm trees. Lights appeared to be hanging everywhere! In Magborou, we lived our nights in darkness except for the light from the fire or the few kerosene lamps we owned.

"May I stay with you?" Fatmata asked in a low voice. She was a little taller than me, I could see as we stood side by side, and a bit heavier. I guessed she was about 20.

Fatmata led me to the pam-pam, a boat similar to the long wooden canoe men used in Magborou to fish. I spied a few other pam-pams in the water, sunk down with only their helms sticking out.

"No," I cried. "I can't go. It will sink. I'm sure it will!"

I had never been in a boat before, and I knew there was no way I could swim without my hands.

Fatmata assured me that everything would be all right. "I'll hold you the entire time," she said. "We will get to the other side safely."

We were the last people to board. The boat moved smoothly, and my apprehension lifted as I watched the lights of the city dance over the water. I had always wanted to visit Freetown, because the adults in the village talked about how big and exciting it was.

Once we landed, ECOMOG soldiers led us to another truck. The vehicle made a singing noise as we moved through the streets of Freetown; I know now it was a siren. In the West, ambulances blare to tell drivers to get out of the way. But in

Freetown, the people crowded onto the streets didn't seem to notice. They walked right in front of that truck, not bothering to step aside. If I had been healthy, I could have reached the hospital more quickly on foot.

When we arrived at the front gate of the hospital, a woman in a nurse's uniform directed us to a building at the end of the big complex of hospital wards.

"She's telling us to go there for the night," Fatmata said. "Don't you worry, little one, I will stay with you tonight."

The stench from the building reached me before I even walked inside—blood, vomit, and sweat. The auditorium was crowded with people lying on the bare cement floor. Blood was everywhere. As I passed through the door with Fatmata by my side, I felt like one of Mohamed's ghosts on the lookout for a healthy body to possess. But this building held no one healthy; everyone was sick. When I sat down, I immediately threw up.

I was among the first to be treated the next morning. Some nurses took me to a bright white room with a huge light hanging from the ceiling. One of the nurses explained it was an operating room.

The doctor, a man with a gruff voice, wore a long white coat and glasses. He spoke Krio, but one of the nurses translated his words into Temne for me. Did I know anyone in Freetown? he asked.

"Yes, my uncle Sulaiman," I replied.

"Do you know where he lives?"

Sulaiman was Marie and my father's youngest brother. I had never visited him, but I knew he was a businessman in

Dovecut, a shopping area in Freetown.

The doctor stuck what looked like a long sewing needle into my arm which he said would put me to sleep. When I awoke, it was nightfall, and Fatmata was by my bedside. I was in a big room lined with beds. It was the girls' ward, Fatmata told me, filled with patients my age and younger. I tried to sit up, but I couldn't; whatever the doctor had given me made me woozy. My arms had been bandaged in bright white material. Not a speck of blood showed through the fabric.

Fatmata held a spoonful of plain white rice up to my mouth. Before I could swallow it, I threw up.

"You need to eat," she said gently. "You need food to give you energy, so we will try again later."

I fell asleep before I could answer.

The next day, when Fatmata came to visit, she told me her uncle had died from his wounds. She had been crying, and I could see she was very sad. When she asked if I'd like to try walking, I nodded yes.

"Then let's go see those boys you know from the truck," she suggested. "They've been asking for you."

As soon as we entered the boys' ward, I spotted Ibrahim. He was lying on one of the many metal cots that filled the room. "Hi, Mariatu," he said, a smile crossing his face. He didn't sit up. Like me, it would take him some time to learn how to do things without hands. "Are you okay?" he asked.

I nodded, blinking back tears.

"Don't you be crying there, Mariatu," I heard Mohamed call. He sat on the edge of the bed directly behind Ibrahim's, his legs dangling, his arms bandaged like mine.

Mohamed had the big fat grin he always wore. Despite the ordeal he had been through, his eyes sparkled.

"I guess we're equal now," he said as I sat down beside him.

"What do you mean?"

"Well, how are we going to wrestle? No one will win."

I don't know where it came from but I laughed and laughed. I felt like that little weaver bird again, but this time I had the feeling I could learn to fly.

CHAPTER 7

"You're pregnant."

I didn't understand what the female doctor in the white coat was saying, though she was speaking Temne. My eyes moved from the doctor's round face to her hands tucked into the pockets of her coat. Abibatu, Marie's younger sister, was standing beside the doctor. She had arrived in Freetown from Port Loko about a week earlier.

"You're pregnant," the doctor said to me again. "You are going to have a baby. Do you understand?"

Abibatu, a large woman with Marie's warm smile, had tears in her eyes. "How did this happen to you?" she asked me.

"I don't know," I muttered. "I don't know." It didn't make any sense.

Since her arrival, Abibatu had taken on many of Fatmata's responsibilities, including helping me bathe. One evening, as she was dipping a cloth into the soapy cold water, she had exclaimed, "Mariatu, your breasts are swollen. When did you last have your time?" Abibatu was referring to my period. Marie had said that I'd eventually get it once every full moon or so, but it wasn't regular yet, and I couldn't remember when it had last come.

"Have you been eating since you came to the hospital?" Abibatu had asked me next.

I shook my head. Anything I tried to eat, including plain white rice or cornmeal, I would immediately throw up. I'd feel sick to my stomach the moment I smelled food coming down the hallway. Sometimes I could swallow a few spoonfuls of the food I carefully took myself, holding the metal spoon in between my bandaged arms. But more often than not I'd motion for Fatmata or Abibatu to bring me a bucket before the spoon even hit my lips.

"I want the doctor to run some tests on you, Mariatu," Abibatu had said worriedly. "I think you might be pregnant."

I wasn't quite sure what *pregnant* meant. But before I could ask her, another woman and another girl with no hands had entered the bathing room. Abibatu helped me out of the tub and dried me off.

When Abibatu and I got back to the girls' ward after learning I was pregnant, Sulaiman and his second wife, yet another Mariatu, were there to greet us. The hospital had tracked him down, and since then he had visited me at least once a day.

Sulaiman was crying, big sobs that seemed to come from deep within his belly. It was shocking. I'd never seen a man cry before. He was also agitated, and as soon as he saw me, he started waving his arms.

"Who did this to you, Mariatu?" he demanded angrily. "I will kill him with my own hands."

I had always liked Sulaiman. Whenever he visited Magborou, he'd bring all the kids candy from Freetown.

Sulaiman didn't talk down to us like many adults did, and he often joined in our games. Now he was scowling and furious. He launched into a tirade, first blaming Marie for what had happened to me, and then starting in on Sierra Leone's president for not stopping the war and on foreigners for not coming to our country's aid. I wasn't always sure what he was talking about. Finally he calmed down, saying he wanted me to come and live with him and his wife. Mariatu stepped forward with a smile to agree.

"You need to get better first," Sulaiman continued. "Your wounds are not quite healed, and you are still on medication to fight infection. I've spoken to the doctors, so I know they expect the outcome to be good. You will be fine—as fine as you can be without hands. And we will help you look after the baby."

When Sulaiman and Mariatu had left, I sat on my bed with Abibatu. "Who did this to you?" she asked, gently rubbing her hands up and down my arms. "Did the rebels give you a baby?"

I was really confused. All I had heard was that babies came from a woman's belly button. When a woman in Magborou had a child inside her, her tummy would swell and then, when she began to waddle like the white-chested ducks from the ponds, the woman would enter the house of the medicine woman. A few other village women would go inside too. Screams soon followed, sometimes lasting for a day and a night. A day or two later, the woman would emerge smiling, holding in her arms a tiny baby.

"No, the rebels did not do this to me," I told Abibatu. "But there must be a mistake. Only women have babies, not girls." My eyes searched her face for some answers.

Abibatu swung her legs around and climbed up beside me. We lay close together as she explained to me how babies were made.

After her explanation, Abibatu left me alone to sleep. I lay very still, thinking over what she had told me about sex and men. And then I knew. I knew what had happened to me.

About a month before we fled to Manarma, we were all in the bush, having heard yet another rumor that the rebels were approaching. It was near the end of Ramadan, and Marie and Alie went back to Magborou ahead of us, to pray and to check that things were safe.

One night after dinner, Ibrahim and Mohamed went to bed early, leaving Adamsay and me by the fire alone. We were sitting quietly under the stars, watching the fire fade, when Salieu approached us.

"Ya Marie and Pa Alie asked me to watch over you girls," he said with a crooked smile. My back stiffened. My body tingled, as if in warning, from head to toe. I didn't like this man, not one bit. There was something about him I feared.

I sat alert and still as the fire turned to glowing coals. I felt too frightened even to move. I said nothing as Adamsay and Salieu talked about Magborou and the village people. Eventually I found the strength to stand up and say good night.

We had made beds for ourselves out of twigs and leaves, and I burrowed into mine. But I couldn't sleep, and for good reason. Not long after, I heard heavy footsteps coming near. I closed my eyes, pretending to be asleep. I hoped it was Adamsay, whose bed was beside mine. But I knew it wasn't.

Salieu lay down beside me. I didn't believe he would do anything to me if I appeared to be sleeping, but he started touching me all over, fondling my breasts and my hair, making his way in between my legs. That's when I sat up.

"What are you doing here? Where is Adamsay?" I shouted.

Salieu just smiled his sinister smile and began touching me some more. I could smell his stale breath and sweat.

"Stop, stop, stop," I yelled. Finally I screamed at the top of my lungs.

A few seconds later, I heard footsteps and then Ibrahim's voice: "What is it? What is it?"

Salieu jumped up, smoothing his cotton shirt and pants. I pulled down my skirt, which was now high above my waist.

"Mariatu is having a nightmare," Salieu, acting like he had just arrived, told Mohamed and Ibrahim when they appeared. He knelt down and gave me a kiss on the forehead. "It's nothing, child," he said. "Go back to sleep. I'll find Adamsay and you two can be together and feel safe."

The next day, we four kids went back to Magborou. Salieu returned to his village to be with his first wife and two young children. I felt a sense of relief, hoping I would never have to see this man again. I was embarrassed and confused about what he had done to me. I told no one.

But soon Salieu started visiting Magborou on a regular basis. He'd come right into our house and ask Alie for a hammer, or Marie for some peppers or a needle and some thread, saying his family was short on supplies because of the war. The whole time he was there, he'd look at me through the slits in the corners of his eyes. My body broke out in goosebumps whenever he was around. I could smell him even after he had left.

"Marie, I need to tell you something," I piped up one afternoon as we were washing some pots by the river. "Salieu is not a good man. Out in the bush, he touched me. He scares me. I don't want to marry him. I never want to be around him again."

I will never forget what happened next. Marie turned, pulled a whipping stick from the ground, and smacked me across the face so hard I was sure I was bleeding. I didn't move. I was in shock.

"Don't you disrespect Salieu," Marie said to me in a hard voice. "He *is* a good man. He would never want to hurt you. He wants to protect you. Don't speak badly of your elders again."

Marie and I went back to washing. I choked back my tears.

A few days later, Salieu came to our house when I was the only one there. The others were all out at the farm.

"Where's Ya Marie?" he asked when he saw me.

"Coming," I lied. I wanted him to think she'd be right back.

"I will wait," he said, sitting down on one of the benches in the parlor.

As I turned to leave, he jumped up and grabbed me by the waist. I started hitting and kicking him.

"If you make any noise," he said coldly, "I will make sure you are punished."

Salieu dragged me down the hall and threw me onto the floor in the room at the back of the hut. He stuffed a piece of fabric into my mouth, tore off my top, and pulled up my skirt so high it covered my face. I could feel him on top of me, then inside of me. Pounding, hurting.

I tried to get loose, to kick, to scratch, but he was too strong. I was a small 12-year-old. He was a big muscleman like Alie.

When Salieu was finished, he pulled my skirt down, smoothed out my hair, and stroked my cheek. He bent down so low that his nose was touching mine. "Don't tell anyone," he said in a harsh, low voice. He pulled the fabric from my mouth and kissed me softly on the lips.

I didn't tell anyone what had happened. I wasn't sure, for one thing, exactly what it was Salieu had done.

Now I knew, and I was going to have a baby.

I sat up in my bed in the girls' ward and looked around. My eyes landed on the blue pills that Abibatu had said were painkillers. They were sitting in a small container on top of the table beside my bed. The other girls in the ward were sound asleep.

I pushed back the sheet, now drenched in sweat, and swung my legs around until I was standing on the bare cement floor. I grabbed the pill bottle between my arms and sat back down on the bed. With my bandages, I tried to pry open the lid. My arms hurt from the pressure, but I didn't give up.

After some concerted effort, the lid opened.

I stopped for a moment to pray.

"Take me, Allah. Take my baby and me. I want to die."

CHAPTER 8

There are times when silence is louder than any voice.

Even though I'd been convinced that the other girls were asleep and that my relatives were gone for the night, staying in Sulaiman's house somewhere in Freetown, I was wrong. Abibatu was still there in the hospital. She had been sleeping on the floor beside another bed, and just as I lifted the bottle to my mouth, she came from out of nowhere and smacked it from my grasp. The tiny blue pills scattered across the floor, making a noise like scurrying mice.

Silence fell again as the last pill stopped spinning. A feeling inside of me, like nothing I had ever felt before, raged forth. An energy bubbled and swirled; I could not control it. I swung around in a fury and lashed out at Abibatu. I shouted at her. I spat at her. I hit her. I kicked her when she tried to grab me.

Everyone in the room was awake by now and gaping at me.

Abibatu stepped back as I threw myself on my bed and then onto the floor. For a moment, I had wanted to kill her. Then there would be no one to stop me from killing myself, and the baby inside of me, too.

I sat on the floor for a long time, my legs pulled up to my

chest, my head perched on my bandaged arms. As my anger subsided, I knew that if I killed Abibatu, there would be one less person in the world who cared about me.

Abibatu rocked me in her arms while I cried and cried.

"I don't want you to kill your baby," she said softly, assuming it was the child I wanted to harm.

But I wanted to die too.

"I have no future," I said to Abibatu. "I have no future," I repeated over and over again.

"Don't talk this way," Abibatu said firmly, spinning me around to face her. "You have many things to live for. Your mother. Your father. Your cousins, grandmother, aunties. They all love you, and you love them."

I shook my head. I didn't want to listen.

The room grew quiet as the other girls returned to sleep. I watched a fly circling one of the kerosene lamps. Like a wave hitting the shore, something washed over me, and I came back to my senses. "You're right," I told Abibatu. "You're right."

Abibatu helped me back into bed and lay down beside me. When I woke up the next day, she was still there, snoring gently.

As the weeks passed, the reality of my situation was never far from my mind. Sometimes all I could think about was Salieu. I hated the baby growing inside me since it reminded me of him. I felt I could almost deal with the horror of what the rebels had done to me. After all, Ibrahim and Mohamed, as well as hundreds of other young people, had also lost their hands. There was some comfort in knowing that we shared the common fate of learning to survive and care for ourselves after such a devastating ordeal. We were all beginning to feed and wash ourselves, even with our injuries. Using the stumps of my arms covered in bandages, I could even brush my teeth and comb my hair. But the baby made me different from them.

One night I had a dream that Salieu came into the girls' ward and sat down beside me on a metal chair.

"Why do you want to kill yourself?" he asked. "Why do you want to kill the baby?"

I said nothing.

"I know you didn't like what I did to you," he said. "And you weren't ready for this. But I love you. And I want you to have this baby for me, because my wife and I only had girls. All I ever wanted was a son."

I turned to him with a tear-stained face. "I hate you," I spat. "I don't want to see you anymore. Go!"

"I'm dead," he said. "But I will always see you, and I will guide you. I also won't let you kill this baby. I know you're going to have a boy. And even though I won't be with that boy, my family will take the baby and look after my son for you."

"How are you going to stop me from killing myself?" I shouted.

"I know what you are trying to do," he responded. "I come here every day to make sure you're okay."

"Why did you do this to me?" I asked then.

"I'm sorry," he replied. "It was a mistake."

"NO! NO! NO!" I yelled. "It was not a mistake. A mistake is putting too much salt on the rice. If what you did to me was a mistake, it was the stupidest mistake you ever made in your life. You should have known better. I will never have a happy life now. I have no hands, and I have a baby growing inside of me that I will never be able to care for. It

might as well die now, because it will die later. I won't be able to look after it. I don't want to see you anymore. I told you to go. Now go!"

I woke with a start. The dream had felt so real that it took a while for me to calm down and realize where I was.

When Abibatu arrived that morning, I described my dream, finally telling her what Salieu had done.

"Ahhh, so you're having a boy," she said. "That will make Salieu very happy."

"*Him* happy!" I responded indignantly. "What about me? What about my happiness?" Back in my old world, I said to her, before the rebels, I had wanted to marry Musa, have four children—two girls and two boys—and wear a beautiful long Africana dress for my wedding. This had been my plan for happiness, I told her. Now it made me sad to remember it.

Until recently, I had thought my cousin Adamsay was dead. I had even told the doctors, nurses, Mohamed, and Ibrahim that the rebels had murdered her. So many people were killed in that attack on Manarma, maybe as many as a hundred, I learned in Freetown. But Adamsay wasn't one of them. The rebels had cut off her hands too. After, she made her way alone through the bush to Port Loko. She was wandering the streets, a dirty and bloodied figure in the crowded markets, when Abibatu's husband stumbled upon her. Abibatu had brought her to Freetown.

When Adamsay and I were reunited on the girls' ward at the hospital, we cried and cried. We held each other for what seemed like hours, until she was taken to the operating room to have her wounds attended to. Since then, we'd spent most of our time together.

By now, we had recovered enough from our injuries to spend our days outside. At first, Adamsay, Mohamed, Ibrahim, and I would wander the hospital grounds, peering into the street over the tall fence.

From what I could see of Freetown, it was a hectic place, with lots of cars and people walking to and from work and the market. It was also hot, hotter than Magborou, probably because of all the buildings and the people crowded together. Air couldn't circulate very well through the dirty city.

Some of the women we saw were dressed in sleek skirts and blouses with buttons and strange collars. While I had never seen clothes like this before, I was even more intrigued by the way the younger women dressed. They wore pants, sometimes so short that their buttocks spilled out. In Sierra Leone, women are prized for having round, full bottoms. We hide our bottoms underneath our long skirts and dresses, because we're brought up to believe we should show no one except our husband this very special part of our body. Our breasts, on the other hand, are what we use to feed our babies. So it's quite normal for a woman to walk around with no shirt on, especially when there is a nursing child nearby. But to show off your bottom! My mouth hung open as I watched these girls over the fence.

"Freetown sure is different from Magborou," I exclaimed once to Mohamed as we observed such a scene.

Mohamed didn't reply. His eyes were trained on the women, and a strange smile transfixed his face. Men, boys, can be funny sometimes!

Another odd sight greeted us when we stepped outside: the

patients themselves. Some of the men, women, and children, bandaged, bruised, and cut, would walk right out of the front gate of the hospital, carrying plastic shopping bags that they thrust toward passersby on the street. Sometimes the Freetown men and women would drop a few leones in a bag. Mostly, though, they would shake their heads and walk right on past.

I soon understood that these patients were begging for money. Almost everyone in the hospital was poor and from the villages. They had ended up in Freetown after the rebels attacked them.

I would soon learn too that kids like me, with no hands, made the best beggars of all. The people of Freetown felt sorry for us, so they gave us more money than they did older people.

The citizens of Freetown all knew about the war. When it had started years before in eastern Sierra Leone, many villagers from the northeast of the country had fled to Freetown, and hundreds of them were now living there, at the hospitals, at places called refugee camps, and right on the streets, sleeping wherever they laid their heads. Later, the fighting had actually reached the city, in January 1999. When they hit Magborou, the rebels were retreating from Freetown.

Ibrahim, Mohamed, Adamsay, and I decided one day to see what begging was like. Soon we were begging every day, though I hated every moment of it.

My hatred toward the world began anew each morning. As the sun lifted, streaming through the windows on my ward, I'd wake with a sinking feeling. My first thoughts were always of my life before Salieu, before the baby, before the rebels came. Mornings reminded me of everything I no longer had.

The day almost always started with Adamsay shaking me before most of the other girls were awake, and whispering: "It's time to go."

As I headed toward the bathroom, I tiptoed around all the sleeping bodies, girls who hadn't discovered yet that they could make a living by begging. I'd wipe a damp cloth over my face and hair. After, I'd straighten out my skirt and top.

Adamsay, Ibrahim, Mohamed, and I would meet at the hospital's front entranceway. We nodded hello but rarely talked as we walked off the hospital grounds. Even at that early hour, the streets were full of people.

On a good day, we could make as much as 10,000 leones, or about three dollars, by pooling our money. The best days were usually Fridays, when we would stand outside the mosque and catch the men on their way out. They had been praying, so they were in a generous mood when they saw us.

Most of the people in the street didn't look at me; they looked down or around me. Sometimes they'd glance at my bandaged arms, where my hands used to be, and shake their heads. Sadness might cross their faces; other times I sensed relief that they themselves had been spared these terrible injuries. The only consistent thing in begging was that very few people dared to look me in the eyes. I learned to fix my gaze on the ground until someone dropped some leones in my black plastic bag. Then I'd raise my eyes to say thank you before quickly lowering them again.

Ibrahim, Mohamed, Adamsay, and I used whatever money we collected to buy a bottle of water from the market to share. Mohamed, being Mohamed, always looked at the bright side of our lives.

"You remember that woman in front of the bus station who talked to you, Mariatu?" he said one day.

I nodded. A tall, skinny woman wearing a navy blue skirt and white blouse had asked me, "Where's your family? Where do you live now? Why did they cut off your hands?"

Like I always did when someone posed these questions, I had thought to myself, "Why do you want to know? It's not as if my story is any different from that of all the other girls in Freetown with no hands because of the war." But I still answered the woman.

"My mom is back in our village," I said. "I live at the hospital now, with my cousins. I don't know why the rebels cut off my hands."

The woman put 25,000 leones into my black bag. It was a fortune, the most money I had ever made in one day by begging.

"I think she wanted to adopt you," Mohamed said now, winking at me. "I know you will be the one, Mariatu," he added. "I know it will be you."

Mohamed meant that I'd be the one among the four of us to be taken in by a rich family. We'd been in the hospital for about a month, and rumors circulated everywhere that there were wealthy people, both in Freetown and in far-off countries, who adopted children who had been injured in the war.

At first, I hadn't known what this word *adoption* meant. But Mohamed explained that it was no different from the way my mother and father had sent me to live with Marie. I allowed myself to daydream a tiny bit about what life would be like as a daughter in another family, a wealthy family: nice clothes, food whenever I wanted it, safety, and sleep-filled nights—all the things we had in Magborou.

Then the horrible words I was greeted with at least once a day broke into my thoughts.

"WHAT HAPPENED TO YOU, BEGGAR GIRL?"

A minibus called a poda-poda was speeding by. A couple of teenage boys leaned out the window, taunting me.

"Can you even feed yourself?" one called out.

"Guess you were in the wrong place at the wrong time," the other yelled. "Now someone will have to look after you for the rest of your life."

I kept my head down, pretending I couldn't hear. But the words were like a knife stabbing into my heart. A thick knot filled my throat. I wanted to kill myself again.

"Why did this have to happen to me?" I raged inside.

CHAPTER 9

I knew that when our bandages came off and were replaced with thin plastic strips, or big Band-Aids, to keep the wounds clean, we would have to leave the hospital. I thought we'd be returning to Magborou, which frightened me. The rebels! What if they were still prowling the countryside? The hospital staff worried about this too. They told Abibatu that we could move to a camp called Aberdeen, set up in Freetown to accommodate people injured in the war.

It wasn't safe to return to Port Loko either, so Fatmata helped Abibatu make the arrangements for our move to Aberdeen. She agreed to live with us for a while and help me when the baby arrived. I was excited. I looked forward to the move and the chance for us all to be sleeping under the same roof.

One rainy day, as Adamsay, Mohamed, Ibrahim, and I returned to the hospital from begging, a young man with a wide smile and a chubby face met us at the front door. He looked familiar, and for good reason: he was Mohamed's uncle Abdul. Mohamed jumped right into his arms.

Abdul lived in Freetown, and he explained that he'd seen Mohamed's name on a Red Cross list of people displaced from their villages that was posted on a billboard in the center of Freetown. When he learned his nephew was in the hospital, he dropped what he was doing and hurried right over.

Abdul reminded me a lot of Mohamed. He told similar jokes, and he was always in a good mood. He started to do for the boys what Fatmata and Abibatu did for me, including preparing their food. He also took them for long walks when Mohamed and Ibrahim weren't out begging.

Abdul was a proud, happy man. He held his head high, with his chest out, and he walked and talked with confidence. When Fatmata was present, though, his eyes stayed downcast, his body slumped, and his speech was sometimes slurred; he always seemed nervous, too, rocking slightly from side to side. Yet when he did manage to look Fatmata's way, the loveliest smile came across his face. Fatmata's personality also changed around Abdul. She was no longer calm and collected. Instead, she became super chatty, talking about everything from the rain to the horrible conditions at the hospital, where many children slept in the hallways because there weren't enough beds. Abdul and Fatmata were falling in love, I realized with a start, and I began to take great interest in this spectacle unfolding in front of me.

One night, after Fatmata had helped me into bed, I snuck out and followed her through the halls. It wasn't difficult to stay hidden, since the hospital was crowded at all hours of the day and night. Abdul was waiting for her near the main entrance. Shyly, they took each other's hands and went out into the Freetown twilight.

Love has a way of being infectious. Watching them, I forgot about my problems for a minute. But as I turned to go, I saw some girls sitting on the floor, their backs up against the wall, their hands amputated like mine. I thought of my own hands, of Salieu, and of the baby growing inside me.

Our impending move to the amputee camp was in the air. Abibatu collected our begging money to buy supplies, including pots, pans, bedding, pepper, and rice. She also used some of the money as bus fare for Abdul. He'd agreed to travel to Manarma and Magborou in search of Marie and Alie. It was a dangerous mission, and Fatmata pleaded with him not to go. None of us had heard anything about my aunt and uncle since the night of the attack. Their names never came up when people in the hospital who'd been caught in the rebel raids on the villages compared stories.

"What happened to Ya Marie and Pa Alie?" I would ask. But no one had an answer. I feared they were dead.

I was overjoyed when my fears proved unfounded. Within a week Abdul returned, bringing Marie and Alie with him. They were dusty and dirty, and much thinner than they had been, but their bodies were intact. We crowded around Mohamed's bed after dinner one night as Marie and Alie explained that they'd hidden in the bush during the attack at Manarma. Afterwards, Alie had gone from village to village, risking his own safety, trying to find out where we were. When we didn't appear, they were scared we'd either been killed or taken into the bush to be soldiers along with the rebels.

At one point during the evening, Adamsay whispered to Marie that I was pregnant. Marie began to wail, her cries echoing through the boys' ward. She cried and cried. Later, I helped her walk back to my ward to spend the night in my bed.

"If I'd only believed you when you told me about Salieu the first time," she sobbed, after I told her about the rape. "If only I had paid more attention. Mariatu, will you ever forgive me?"

I wiped away Marie's tears with my bulky bandages. "Abibatu says we're moving to a nice new home," I consoled her. "Just wait and see: our luck will change."

Just short of two months after I'd arrived at the hospital, we moved to the Aberdeen Amputee Camp. It wasn't what I'd expected. The camp was filthy with litter and with laundry that had fallen from the clotheslines hanging everywhere. There were dogs, and people of all sizes and skin tones, speaking an array of Sierra Leone dialects. The smell of garbage, dirty bodies, and cooking food was sickening.

Our new home was a big tent divided into eight rooms by canvas doors. It housed about five families, and each amputee was assigned one room. I shared mine with Abibatu and Fatmata, who had been living in Freetown with a distant relative. We looked right across at Adamsay's room, where Marie and Alie were also going to sleep. All of the families shared a fire pit outside to cook food. The supplies we got from the camp were bulgur, cornmeal, cornstarch, palm oil, and beans—that was about it.

There was little for anyone in Freetown at the time, let alone us injured kids. Due to the war, farmers could not bring their produce into the city to sell. Meat, cassava, beans, and fresh water were increasingly difficult to find. That responsibility soon fell to the kids. We became the breadwinners in our families through begging.

There was a central place in the camp where everybody would congregate to hear news of the war. We learned there that rebels had crept many times into the camp at night and stolen the scant food that was available. "Be careful," a woman who shared our tent warned us. "Don't travel around the camp alone at night, and sleep with lots of people beside you. If you have a knife or a gun, keep it handy."

I knew that no one in my family had a weapon.

A few people at the camp had tried to grow a garden, we heard, but the rebels had dug it up. There were rumors that the rebels had even invaded the medical supplies storage room and taken all the bandages, pills, medical equipment, and IVs. The rebels sent letters, according to some of the people at the camp, threatening to return. No one was sure if the rumors were true, but it scared us all to hear of the rebels' words. One day someone at the camp read aloud a letter supposedly written by a rebel.

We're coming to get you. We're coming back to finish you all off. The government isn't helping us, but they're helping you, taking care of you. So we are going to come back and chop off the hands of anyone who still has theirs, including the hands of the people looking after you. Why? Because you don't deserve the help from the government, the money they are giving you, the clothes and food. But we do.

The letter chilled me to the bone, reigniting all my terrible memories. In fact, the words were a lie, because the government wasn't helping us. There were more than 400 of us at the camp who didn't have hands. At least four times that many people, mostly family members like Abibatu, Marie, and Alie, had moved there to look after the injured. The camp wasn't really big enough for all of us—it was about the size of the soccer stadium in Freetown.

Our relatives cooked for us and fed us. The camp received a shipment of flour once a month that was doled out to the first few hundred people in line. Our family had to show up early or we got nothing. The begging money my cousins and I collected paid for most of our food and clothes. On the days we didn't earn much by begging, we ate nothing, or just a few spoonfuls of rice. We were starving.

About a month after we moved to the camp, Abdul appeared one evening after dinner. Now that Mohamed and Ibrahim had Alie to help care for them, Abdul had settled back into his old life, running a small shop in Freetown. He said he wanted to tell the family something special and asked if we could gather the following night.

Marie tried to prepare a nice dinner for Abdul. She collected the few leones we kids had saved from begging and went to the market to buy some fish. We all suspected we were about to have a celebration.

After we had eaten our meal, Abdul told us the news. He was sitting beside Fatmata, and he stroked her hand as he spoke. "Fatmata and I are getting married!" he announced. Fatmata lowered her head shyly as Abdul kissed her on the cheek.

Everyone jumped up. The women hugged and kissed Fatmata. The men patted Abdul on the back and shook his hand. Their faces radiant with happiness, they told us of their plans to hold the ceremony at Fatmata's uncle's home in

Freetown. It would be too dangerous for us all to travel to Port Loko, where Fatmata's family lived. They wanted to marry right away, that week if they could.

But as we learned after Abdul and the other men had left, there was one problem.

"You've been waiting your entire life since your Bondo initiation for this day," Abibatu said to Fatmata with a big smile.

Fatmata lowered her head again. "I'm sorry," she said quietly. "But I have not been initiated."

"What!" exclaimed Abibatu. "Well, you can't marry until you are. We will do it immediately, here at the camp."

Most of the Sierra Leonean girls I know have been initiated in what we call the Bondo Secret Society. I had my own initiation when I was about nine. In the week leading up to it, I was forbidden to go to the farm or to do any chores, including helping Marie to cook or clean.

"Just relax," Marie told me. "Bondo happens only once in a girl's lifetime. Go for walks, braid your hair with pretty beads, and take long naps in the afternoon."

The Bondo is seen as a rite of passage for young girls, and boys and men are banned from coming near where the Bondo initiation takes place.

The day before my initiation, Marie prepared some elaborate rice dishes with fish, goat, beans, and spices that she made only for special occasions, such as Eid.

The next day, she took Adamsay and me to the river, where we joined a group of about eight other girls. Accompanying each girl was her mother or auntie. We were each handed a new bar of white soap. That was very unusual, as we always shared soap among the family. I'd never been given a bar of soap especially for me. "Wash better than you've ever washed before," Marie instructed us.

After a long soak in the river, Adamsay and I donned matching Africana outfits. We headed into the bush to join the digba, the woman who leads the initiation, who was already there waiting for us.

A hut had been erected especially for the other girls and me, and it would be our home. We'd be allowed to leave it only to use the toilet, and before we went outside, we had to paint our faces and bodies in white, chalky paint. The paint was to symbolize our purity, and the transition from child to girl or woman. Until the end of the initiation, we could only be seen in public covered in this paint. Living in the hut was fun, like summer camp for girls in North America. We stayed up late into the night, gossiping and telling stories. The secret society made us as close as sisters.

There was only one part of the Bondo that I disliked, and it happened on our first night in the bush. After we'd eaten the delicious dishes prepared by the women, I was told to lie down on the dirt floor on a piece of cloth. Despite the fact that there were older girls being initiated with me, the digba had identified me as the karukuh, the girl with spiritual powers, so I'd been chosen to go first in the initiation. My skirt was lifted high over my waist. Some of the aunties and mothers held down my feet and arms while the other women there, including Marie, drummed and sang. A cloth was placed over my eyes.

I felt the digba cut my vagina. The pain was excruciating,

and I screamed as I struggled to break free. I even bit one of the women as she held me down.

When the Bondo, or cutting, was done, I had to sit in a chair with strips of cotton between my legs to stop the bleeding. I watched as Adamsay and the other girls from my village went through the same ordeal. We were all in pain for days afterwards, but at least sharing the experience let us laugh about how awful we felt.

During the four months we lived in the hut, the women from the village taught us homemaking, including cooking and sewing. We learned how to cook meals that would cure certain ailments, and how to use herbs to treat coughs and fevers. At the end of our time there, we returned to the village for a great feast, during which all of us danced.

Fatmata's Bondo initiation happened not in the bush but in one of the rooms at the camp. The ceremony lasted only one night, as Fatmata already knew how to cook, sew, and cure ill-nesses. In the West, this practice of cutting, known as female genital mutilation, is highly criticized. But in Sierra Leone, girls and women who are not initiated are considered outsiders.

The wedding was held about a month after Fatmata's initi-ation. An imam offered the blessing and read a sura, a passage from the Quran. We celebrated with a nice dinner of rice and goat. And that was it—Abdul and Fatmata were married!

Fatmata was so happy that day, which made me happy too. She was like a gift from God to me, coming into my life at one of my darkest moments, caring for me in Freetown until my family arrived. She had become my mom, my sister, and my friend from the first moment fate brought us together in the back of that army truck in Port Loko.

I was sad after Fatmata's wedding. I even cried a little. I wanted to celebrate her marriage for days, weeks if I could, like we did when couples wed back at Magborou. But I guess that's what happens during a war: occasions that make people feel happy aren't as frequent.

CHAPTER 10

One late afternoon, after begging in the streets, I rounded the corner to my tent to see Musa standing there, talking to Marie. I was heavy by now with the baby. My walk was a waddle, like the women I knew back in Magborou just before they gave birth. I walked down to the clock tower in Freetown, which was the busiest part of the city and a good place to beg, with my cousins each morning, but I couldn't keep up with them on the journey home, often falling so far behind that Freetown was shrouded in darkness by the time I made it to the camp. Recently, I had started leaving the city as soon as Freetown became thick with afternoon haze.

When I saw Musa, I stopped in my tracks. I was paralyzed. A part of me wanted to run away. Another part of me wanted to fly into his arms.

Musa noticed me before I could make a decision. His face opened into a wide smile. "Hello, Mariatu. How are you?" he called out.

I stood quietly as Musa wrapped his arms around me. The scent of his warm body reminded me of our times together at the farm, holding hands under the hot noonday sun.

I despaired at the thought I'd never be able to hold his hand again.

"Do you want to go for a walk?" Musa suggested, standing back.

I shrugged. "Sure."

As we strolled around the camp, Musa told me about his life since we'd last seen each other. He and his mother had escaped their village before the rebels burned it down. They had made their way to Freetown and were living in the cramped apartment of relatives along with another family.

So many villagers were now streaming into Freetown to avoid the rebels that neighbors in the city often knew each other from the provinces. One of Musa's neighbors had fled Manarma just before the attack. He told Musa that he'd heard afterwards that four cousins from Magborou had had their hands amputated there. Worrying that I was one of them, Musa had come immediately to the camp.

By the time we circled back to the tent, Mohamed, Ibrahim, and Adamsay were having their evening meal of rice and groundnut soup.

"Do you want to eat?" I asked Musa.

He shook his head, so I motioned for him to follow me inside. We sat side by side on my straw mat. "Tell me what happened to you, Mariatu," he pleaded. He listened patiently as my story tumbled out.

Musa cried when I was finished. "If only I had stayed with you," he said, "we could have escaped the rebels together. I love you."

My body stiffened. His words echoed in my head. "I love

you, too," I wanted to tell him. But I didn't. I didn't want Musa to love me anymore. My body slumped forward as I wrapped my arms underneath me.

"Musa," I said in a voice drained of emotion. "I think you need to find someone else."

"No," Musa cried out. He pulled me into his arms, starting to rock me, but I pushed him away.

"Go," I said to him. "Go, and don't come back. I don't want you to see me anymore, not like this." I held up my arms, then rubbed my pregnant belly. "I want you to find a normal girl and have a normal life. And I want you to remember me for who I used to be, what I used to look like."

"I want *you*, Mariatu."

"Musa," I shouted, "I'm telling you. Don't love me anymore!"

"But I want to be with you," he stammered. "I want you to name your baby Musa and come and be my wife one day, like we promised."

I pushed him away from me. "It will never happen. I want you to go and never come back."

Musa continued to protest, but with every word I withdrew further. I stopped listening. I lost interest in even arguing with him. I let him ramble on and on until he stopped.

When silence finally filled the tent, Musa kissed me on the forehead and slowly got up.

"I will come back," he said. "I will make you see that we can still be together."

I didn't even look at him as he left the tent.

Musa came back twice before the baby was born. Both times it was just as the sun was setting for the night and I had returned from begging. Both times I said I was too tired to talk. I left him by the fire, conversing with Ibrahim and Mohamed, and went into the tent alone. I didn't cry. Every time a thought of Musa popped into my head, I shook it away. Yet when I heard Musa call goodbye, I felt a great emptiness inside me.

On a morning not long after Musa's third visit, I woke very early. It was still dark outside. My clothes were dripping wet from perspiration, and I felt cold and shaky despite the heat. As I rolled over to get up, pain surged through my abdomen and down my legs and arms.

"OUUUCH," I yelled. "OUUUCH." Writhing around on my mat, I screamed for Abibatu, Fatmata, and Marie.

Abibatu kept a small basket of clean white strips torn from sheets by the side of my mat. She intended to use them when she and the others helped deliver my baby, she said. Fatmata had been gathering secondhand clothes for the child, mostly from Father Maurizio, a bald-headed and almost always smiling Italian priest who worked at the camp.

Marie rushed into the room. She felt my stomach, then examined me. "There is something wrong," she said. "You're not dilating."

Marie ran to get the camp nurse, who gave the same diagnosis. "Mariatu will have to deliver the baby at the hospital," the nurse said. "I'll call for the ambulance."

We waited several hours for the ambulance, which was a Red Cross jeep, and it seemed to take just as long to navigate the busy Freetown streets. By the time we got to the maternity hospital, it was noon. My contractions were coming fast and furiously.

A female doctor there explained that my birth canal was too small. "And the baby is big," she said. "There's no room for the baby to come out. You'll need to have an operation called a C-section." She ran her finger along my stomach to show me where she'd make the incision.

The last thing I recall is the doctor sticking a needle into my arm.

Many hours later, I woke in a bright room, light streaming in through a big open window. I felt listless as I watched some dust dancing in the sun's rays. My eyelids were starting to close again when I suddenly remembered where I was, and why. As I tried to sit up, I was greeted with more pain. Pulling the sheet away, I saw that my stomach was taped and bandaged.

I started to cry, and the other girl in the room called out for help.

Abibatu hurried in to comfort me. After a moment Marie arrived, carrying my baby.

"It's a boy," said Abibatu, reaching over to take the child.

A boy, just as Salieu had predicted in my dream. The baby was swathed in a blue blanket. All I could see were his round face and matted black hair. He was cooing. With one look at that little face, all my anger disappeared. The baby looked like I imagined an angel would, with his soft, chubby cheeks. "I can take care of this baby," I thought. "I can even love this child."

"What do you want to name him?" Marie asked me.

"Abdul," I blurted out.

I hadn't thought about it in advance, but I knew instantly

that this baby would be named Abdul, after Fatmata's Abdul, Mohamed's uncle.

Abibatu held Abdul in one hand as she helped prop me up into a sitting position with pillows behind me. She shaped my arms into a cradle, then placed the baby in them.

I'd never felt such love in my heart.

Abdul made sucking sounds, puckering his lips like a fish.

"What's he doing?" I giggled.

"I think he wants to be fed," Abibatu replied.

"Come on, little mommy," Marie joked. She held Abdul as Abibatu pulled up my top.

"What are you doing?" I demanded.

"You're going to breast-feed your child," Marie told me. She put Abdul back in my arms, pushed his face onto my breast, and fastened his mouth onto my nipple.

My sensations of love soured as anger washed over me.

"Can't one of you feed him?" I asked Marie and Abibatu. No one had told me this would be my responsibility.

Marie laughed. "Mariatu," she said, "my breasts are old. There is no milk left in them. And Abibatu has never had a child. She can't give milk. Only you can."

I stayed in the hospital for about two weeks. The doctors wanted to make sure that my stomach was healing properly and that I was breast-feeding Abdul before letting me return to Aberdeen.

"There are lots of diseases at the camp," a nurse told me. "Malaria, dysentery, colds, and flus. You need to be healthy so that your milk will give Abdul a shot at surviving those bad conditions."

"Food is scarce in the camp, so it's important that you try to eat as much as you can while you're here," Abibatu added.

Some people at the camp were so thin that you could see their ribs through their T-shirts. They coughed and wheezed as they walked. Some of the amputees had died from their wounds, a few right in their tents. It was common at night to hear someone screaming in pain. But I had become used to the sounds. I hadn't realized that many of the diseases at the camp could be passed from one person to another.

Abdul slept beside my bed in a small metal crib. Abibatu, Marie, and Fatmata felt that the baby and I would bond better if we were together all the time, but that never happened. Abdul would cry in that crib and I couldn't move. I'd just stare at him until one of the women put him on my breast to feed. I didn't rock Abdul in my arms. I didn't sing lullabies to him. I didn't talk to him. I don't know why.

When I first saw the gaping scar on my stomach from the C-section, I felt like vomiting. All I could think was: "What else? What other deformity will befall my body?"

After the nurse removed my stitches, I headed straight to the washroom down the hall. In the privacy of a stall, I tried to rip off my bandages with my arms and teeth. My plan was to punch myself in the stomach until I bled to death. I couldn't get the bandages off, though. Eventually I gave up and rested my head against the wall.

Since finding out I was pregnant, I'd endured serious bouts of depression, followed by moments of extreme happiness in which I forgot all about the war. Fatmata and Abdul's marriage was one such occasion. I'd felt hopeful then. I dreamt that one day it would be me wearing a beautiful Africana wedding dress. But as my gaze floated to the ceiling in that washroom stall, I wondered if I would ever have one of those happy moments again.

CHAPTER 11

Ibrahim, Mohamed, and Adamsay were very nice to me when I returned to the camp, taking turns holding the baby and asking me what childbirth was like. "I was asleep for it all" was my answer. Everyone gave me extra food, particularly vegetables. Over dinner, I'd lose myself listening to my cousins talk about their day, kids they'd met on the street while begging or something funny that had happened, like someone getting beaten up for stealing a pineapple from one of the vendors. Then Abdul would start whimpering. My cousins would go elsewhere as Marie or Abibatu passed the baby to me. The shadows cast by the fire couldn't conceal the frustration that showed on my face.

Begging was completely off-limits for me, even though I desperately wanted to go. I tried everything to get Marie to give me permission. "We need more food, because you're giving me so much extra," I'd plead.

"No."

Mohamed made me feel worse by poking fun at my situation. "You're a grown woman now, Mariatu," he'd laugh. "Why would you want to hang out with us young kids? Stay home with the adults. Feed your baby and we'll look after you."

The longing to join my cousins became so strong that one morning, after I'd finished breast-feeding Abdul, I handed him back to Fatmata, stood up, and declared: "I'm going with the others tomorrow!"

"You can't," Marie protested. "Abdul needs you."

Abibatu stepped in. "I'm worried. You and Abdul aren't bonding like a mother and child should. He spends most of his time with us," she said, pointing to herself, Marie, and Fatmata.

"I will go with Mariatu," said a voice from the entranceway to our tent. Startled, we all turned to look. Standing there, her hands on her big hips, was Mabinty.

Mabinty was an older lady who lived in one of the other rooms. She hadn't been injured in the war, but rebels had burned down her home. She'd walked to Freetown along with many others from her village. She missed her daughter, who lived in her husband's village in the north of Sierra Leone. "If I could get to her village without fear that the rebels might ambush me," Mabinty would moan, "I'd go tomorrow."

The rebels were still invading villages, though not as often as they had in the past. The number of casualties reaching Freetown was diminishing. Still, ECOMOG forces warned Sierra Leoneans not to travel on the main roads or through the western regions of the country in case of sudden attacks.

Mabinty didn't have much to do at the camp, so she occasionally helped care for Abdul by bathing him in one of the big plastic tubs or rocking him to sleep as she sang Temne songs.

"I will go with Mariatu," Mabinty said again. "I'll look after Abdul while she joins her friends. In my village, I cooked, sewed, and helped look after lots of babies. I was a grand-mother to many children. Now I do nothing but sit around and watch the younger women cook."

I ran up to Mabinty and hugged her. "Thank you! Thank you!" I said over and over again.

Marie, Fatmata, and Abibatu threw up their arms at the same time.

"What are we going to do with you, Mariatu?" Marie exclaimed.

The next day, my begging routine started again. Adamsay would wake me in the mornings. If Abdul was still sleeping, I'd rush outside and brush my teeth before waking him. After I'd fed him, we all left the camp together, Adamsay, Ibrahim, Mohamed, Mabinty, Abdul, and me.

Adamsay and I often split off from the boys, as people in Freetown gave more money to girls. We'd ask people for leones all the way down to the clock tower in the middle of Freetown, and then all the way back to the camp. Mabinty, holding Abdul, remained close. When he was hungry, the three of us would go behind a market stall or down an alleyway, away from the other kids. I'd sit on the dirty ground and breast-feed; Mabinty stood in front of me, blocking any onlooker's view. I'd give Abdul back to Mabinty for another hour or so of begging before he indicated he needed me again, by puckering his lips and softly crying.

Such were my days for a while. One afternoon, quite by chance, I was holding Abdul while Mabinty was off talking to another older woman. I was standing impatiently, pacing back and forth, when a man dropped 40,000 leones (about $12) into my black plastic shopping bag. It was the most money I'd ever earned at one time.

"Poor child," he said to me. He patted Abdul on the head before walking on.

"He took pity on you," Mabinty said after I explained excitedly what had happened.

"Why?" I wondered.

"Because you have not only yourself to feed, but Abdul," she said. "Watch. You start carrying that child and you'll get more money than anybody."

Indeed, passersby always singled me out when I held Abdul. From then on, I earned more money each day than all of my cousins combined.

When Abdul was several months old, a camp official came to our tent one night looking for me. He explained to me in Krio, which I now understood from hearing it all the time in Freetown, that some foreign journalists were coming to the camp the next day. They wanted to interview and take pictures of amputees from the war. Would I come the next morning, with Abdul, to the main part of the camp to meet them?

I was puzzled. "What is a journalist?" I asked.

"Someone who will tell your story to people in other countries," the man replied.

"What do these people want with Mariatu?" Marie asked him. "She's just a poor village girl."

"Not anymore," the official said. "Her village was ruined and the rebels hurt her badly. The world needs to know about the war in Sierra Leone."

Abibatu pressed him further. "What will Mariatu get out of this?"

"Maybe someone will read about her and send her money, try to help her," the man replied. Apparently several youth in the camp had people from foreign countries sending them money and supplies. "Some of the children are even going to live in the West, in wealthy countries where there are no wars, all because journalists are telling the world about our problems."

At first I said no, thinking of all the money I'd be missing by not begging. But Marie and Fatmata encouraged me to go.

"Someone might hear about you, Mariatu, and give you money," Fatmata said.

The next morning, I marched to the center of the camp with Abdul in my arms, a little angry at letting my cousins go off to Freetown without me. I sat down with a huff on a bench, well back from where I could see the camp official and the journalists talking.

When the official spotted me, he jogged over, smiling. He led me to a big table where four people were seated. For a moment I was speechless. For the first time in my life, I was looking at blue eyes and green eyes, yellow hair and brown hair, and these men and women had the lightest skin I had ever seen.

A woman with short red hair put her hand on my shoulder. "Hello," she said in Krio. That impressed me, since Marie and Alie had told us that foreign people didn't speak Temne, Krio, or Mende, the three main languages of Sierra Leone. The woman was pretty, and she made me feel at ease.

"Can you tell them about what happened to you?" the camp representative jumped right in.

I didn't know where to begin, so I sat quietly, thinking. The lady with the red hair said something to the representative, who turned to me. "She wants to know if you are with your family?"

"Yes," I replied. That was an easy question.

The representative translated another question from the woman. "Do you need anything?"

"Vegetables, clean water, soap, new clothes, dishes." I don't know where my answer came from, but I found myself reciting a long list of everything we didn't have at the camp that we'd had back at Magborou.

I then broke into my story, or at least a small portion of it: "My name is Mariatu. I am a victim of the rebel attack on Manarma. Child soldiers held me hostage for ten hours and then cut off my hands. I now live at Aberdeen with my cousins Adamsay, Ibrahim, and Mohamed, who were also in the Manarma attack. They don't have hands either."

"How old is your baby?" the red-haired woman asked.

"His name is Abdul," I replied. "He's five months old."

My first interview with the media lasted about 15 minutes. The representative then led the journalists on a tour of the camp, asking me to follow behind. At one point he directed me to stand still, with Abdul in my arms, so that the photographers could take pictures of me. I remember it well. My bare feet were caked in mud; a dog barked wildly in the background; behind me was a clothesline.

The camp official slipped a few leones into my arms and said he would call for me again.

It would be many years before I read the articles written about me that day and in the days to come. Every one of them would come back to haunt me. The journalists all said the rebels had raped me and that I had conceived Abdul during the attack on Manarma.

CHAPTER 12

"He's sick, Mariatu," Marie said. "He's very sick. The doctor says Abdul needs a blood transfusion or he might die."

Abdul was now about 10 months old. Over the past few weeks, his stomach had become swollen, so swollen he looked as if he was carrying a small baby inside. At first I thought he was getting fat from my milk. But he really wasn't taking in as much milk as he had when he was younger. He'd also started crying more and more.

A nurse at the camp clinic gave Abdul a needle with some vitamins that were supposed to make him healthy. We went to see her every day, but the needle wasn't helping. Abdul's stomach got bigger and his face grew puffy. His legs had lost their baby fat. He was so skinny in some places and so fat in others that he looked distorted.

When the nurse first told me that Abdul was suffering from malnutrition, I started eating as much as I could, hoping I could make my milk more nourishing. I ate so many spoonfuls of rice that I felt I'd throw up. I stopped going out to beg with Adamsay and Mabinty, and spent all my time with Abdul at the camp. I'd cradle him in my arms until he fell asleep. I even sang to him—very softly, since I didn't want anyone else to hear my bad singing voice.

But nothing I did seemed to make a difference. One day, the nurse said we needed to take Abdul to the hospital.

Abibatu, Marie, and Fatmata came with me. We were back at Connaught, but in a different ward—this one was for babies—than where I stayed when I first arrived in Freetown.

"If Abdul dies, it will be all my fault," I thought. "I should have loved him more." In between being angry at myself, I tried to figure out how I could get enough money for the blood transfusion he needed. "I could go out and beg," I said to myself, "pleading with anyone who walks my way. I could get my cousins to do the same. We could steal the money from the fabric salesman."

Then a rational thought poked its way in. Father Maurizio, the Italian priest who had given me all of Abdul's clothes: I would go to see him. Fatmata, Abibatu, and Marie approved of my plan. I kissed Abdul on the forehead and then I was off.

I ran faster than I ever had, out of the hospital, through the packed, market-lined streets of Freetown, down toward the ferry, and straight to the compound where Father Maurizio lived.

"I need your help," I gasped when I saw him. Father Maurizio looked at me wide-eyed as I blurted out my reason for coming.

"Okay, Mariatu," the priest said. "Let me see what I can do."

Father Maurizio provided shelter at his mission for boys and girls who were separated from their families. He had access to wealthy people back in Italy who shipped him clothes and other necessities and wired him money for various programs.

The priest offered me a cup of water, then asked one of his staff to drive me back to the hospital.

"This is all my fault," I cried out to Father Maurizio just before we pulled away. "If I had loved Abdul more, he would want to live. If he dies, it's because my lack of love killed him."

Father Maurizio showed up at the hospital several hours later. He had found the money through an Italian donor. The doctors did the transfusion immediately, but afterwards Abdul was worse than before. He lay weakly in my arms, his big brown eyes gazing off into the air. He didn't even cry to tell me he was hungry.

Three days later, Abdul's almost-weightless body fell completely still. His breathing grew shallow. Every so often his eyes would blink as if in slow motion. I sat clutching him tightly.

"I think it's time," Marie said gently, taking Abdul from my arms. She motioned for me to go outside and shut the door behind me.

As I walked down the hall, I kept my eyes focused directly forward, blocking out the other babies on the ward. Every time I looked at them, all I could see was Abdul's face.

Later that day, back at the camp, I went straight to my room. I lay down on the mat I slept on. Whenever anyone tried to talk to me, I'd respond with a gruff "Leave me alone." For the first few days, I got up only to use one of the urinals in the camp. On my way back, I'd grab a few bites of rice, then return to my room and my mat.

My family held a funeral ceremony for Abdul in the camp's mosque. The imam recited a prayer, and one by one my family asked for blessings. I sat motionless, listening but not really hearing. Whenever we were supposed to recite a passage from the Quran, I did so under my breath.

"Allah," I said in my head. "Help make me a better person."

In the weeks that followed, I spent all my time sleeping. Abibatu, Fatmata, and Marie tried to console me many, many times, bringing me plates of rice and vegetables that I'd push away. Marie told me stories about Magborou. "We'll go back one day," she said. "You wait and see. We'll be back in Magborou very soon."

Abibatu often scolded me. "You have to pick yourself up, or else what's the point of living? Those rebels should have killed you right then and there."

Fatmata, who, along with Abdul, was living part of the time at the camp now, took a different approach. "There are still lots of things to be hopeful for, Mariatu."

"Like what?" I grumbled. All I could see before me was a life of begging and depending on others for my survival. The best thing I could do for my family would be to move away. But where?

My sleep was haunted by images of Abdul. I'd have conversations with myself in my dreams: "Abdul was a person. He understood I did not love him. He knew I did not want him, so he left the world."

I'd hear Abdul crying and I'd wake with a start. Relief swept through me, until I realized I'd been dreaming. A frequent dream was feeling Abdul lying on my stomach. I'd awake hugging him, only to find he was not there.

Abibatu and Marie collected all of Abdul's clothes and toys and gave them back to Father Maurizio. Soon all that was left to remind me of him was the long scar on my stomach. When this knowledge hit me, I cried for nearly half a day. I cried until I had nothing left in me, then fell into one of my fitful sleeps.

In the dream that followed, Salieu came to me a second time. He sat down beside me, as he had in the dream after I first learned I was pregnant.

"Are you mad at me?" I asked him.

"Of course not," he answered.

"But I killed Abdul."

"No, you didn't," he replied. "You were too young, Mariatu. What I did to you was selfish. I am sorry for the pain I have caused you. Abdul is with me."

Abdul suddenly appeared, sitting on Salieu's lap. He was wearing such a big smile, I could see his two bottom teeth; they had come in just before he got sick. Abdul looked like he had before the illness, with his fat legs and arms, normal-sized stomach, and round, happy eyes.

"Everything will be fine from now on," Salieu said, standing up with Abdul in his arms. "Don't blame yourself again for Abdul's death."

It was the last time I ever saw Salieu.

I wish I could have taken comfort from Salieu's words. But I couldn't. I hated him for what he had done to me, and I missed Abdul. Nonetheless, the morning after my dream, I did feel a lightness I hadn't experienced in a while. I woke early, washed my face, changed into a clean T-shirt and wrap skirt, brushed my teeth with a chewing stick, and went down to the clock tower with Adamsay. I didn't say much to her, though she tried to talk to me. When a businessman dropped some leones into her bag, she ran off immediately to the market to buy me a mango. She held it up, but I shook my head. "You eat it," I sighed. I didn't feel I deserved her kindness.

I trudged along the streets, my black plastic shopping bag held low by my side. I didn't make any money that day. But the next day I lifted my bag a little higher. And by the day after that, I was talking to Adamsay again.

"I got accepted into a program," she confided as we walked home one afternoon. "I might be going to Germany."

I was excited for her. I was happy for all the children at the camp who were taking part in programs with foreign nonprofit groups. The camp official had been right when he said that people in the West were becoming interested in Sierra Leone.

"It isn't an adoption program," Adamsay continued, sighing a little. "I'll only be going to Germany for a little while, to go to school."

"Where is Germany?" I asked her.

"Germany is in Europe," she replied, pointing north, as if this place called Germany was just beyond Freetown's mountains. "It's supposed to be green."

"Oh," I said, looking down. I'd suddenly realized what her leaving would mean to me.

"Don't worry," Adamsay said. She stopped and wrapped her big arms around me. She was about to let go when I found myself pulling her in tight. I held on to her for a long time, burrowing my face into her soft, fleshy shoulder. She smelled like grass, and that reminded me of Magborou. I wanted to go back there, back to the time when Adamsay, Mariatu, and I would play with stilts and make mud pies that we'd try to get Marie to eat.

The following Saturday, another girl named Mariatu who

lived at the camp popped by to see me. Mariatu was the same age as me. She looked like me, too, and she had no hands. Rebels had attacked her when they invaded Freetown.

We didn't go begging on the weekends, since the business-people didn't work then. The people who filled Freetown's bustling streets on Saturdays and Sundays were mostly poor villagers from the countryside escaping the war. They would ask *us* for money, so it was pointless to go to the city. Weekends were spent hanging around the camp, cleaning the few clothes we owned, grinding cassava, and hearing about the war from others.

I knew this other Mariatu quite well, because she often joined Adamsay and me for begging. Now she sat down beside me as I finished breakfast.

"Victor thinks it would lift your spirits if you came out to the theater troupe," she announced.

Mariatu had tried to get me to join the camp's theater troupe before I gave birth to Abdul. She'd even taken me to one of their rehearsals when I was about eight months pregnant.

The troupe had about 25 members, all of them war amputees. They met every Saturday and Sunday in the center of the camp. Some of the members had lost a foot, others had no hands. Most of the members were around my age, but there were some older men and women too. When I saw them rehearse that first time, they were doing a play about the war. Mariatu played herself, a young girl from a small village in northwestern Sierra Leone who'd come to Freetown with her mother in the hope of avoiding the rebels. Two boys played the parts of the child soldiers who maimed her. Their lines were all too familiar.

"Go to the president," one boy said.

"Ask him for new hands," said the other boy.

After the rehearsal, Mariatu had introduced me to Victor, who'd organized the troupe. Victor knew far too well the experiences many of us had endured. While the rebels had not harmed him, many of his friends and some of his family had been killed in the attack that destroyed his village.

The script brought back too many bad memories for me, so I'd politely told Mariatu and Victor that I couldn't join the troupe. "I will need to look after my baby," I had said. "But thank you for asking me. Maybe some other time."

Some other time was now, and Mariatu was not taking no for an answer.

"It will be good for you to think about things other than Abdul," she coaxed.

"But I'm no good at acting," I complained.

"Then you can sing!" Mariatu retorted.

"I'm no good at singing either," I said, shaking my head.

"I know you can dance," she persisted. "Just show me a Sierra Leonean girl who can't dance!"

Now I really couldn't argue. Every village girl in Sierra Leone learns to dance as soon as she can walk. It was what we did almost every night by the fire. My friends and I would don grass skirts and some Africana beads and take turns dancing in twos and threes, while some of the boys from Magborou drummed and the rest of the village sang and clapped.

"Okay," I said to Mariatu. "I'll come and watch you today. I have nothing else to do anyway. But I'm not joining!"

After I had finished my breakfast and washed up, Mariatu

and I wove our way through the tents. When we reached the center of the camp, the theater troupe was just about to perform a skit on HIV/AIDS.

I'd heard mention of the virus that was killing people in Sierra Leone, but no one in my family had it, so we had never talked about it. I had no idea how you acquired HIV/AIDS until I watched the skit that afternoon. The plot involved a funeral ceremony for a woman who had just died from AIDS. While the mourners stood motionless, two older members of the troupe, a man and a woman, explained that HIV/AIDS is acquired through sexual intercourse. When they were done speaking, the play resumed.

Mariatu's role was that of the bereaved daughter. Mariatu was good at acting. Her tears seemed real.

"She was a good woman who cared about her family," her character wailed.

When the funeral ceremony ended, the whole cast came out and sang a song about HIV/AIDS.

It's killing all of Africa. How do we stop it? Only we can stop it! Be faithful to your wife, husband, or partner.

When the skit was over, Mariatu and Victor approached me.

"So you finally came out," Victor said with a smile, punching me gently on the shoulder.

"I just wanted to watch," I said.

"But we'd love to have you in the troupe," he said. Victor was a tall, handsome man with an oval face and very short hair. When he smiled, his eyes drooped downwards slightly, giving him an innocent look. Even though I had only met him once or twice before, I'd liked him right away.

"I've been through a few things recently," I confessed. "I don't know if I am up to acting, singing, and dancing yet."

"I know about the baby and his death," he said kindly. "I wanted you to join the troupe a long time ago, but I realized it was too soon. Having a baby at twelve years of age is very hard."

I wanted to tell Victor that I had killed Abdul, that I was a mean person and he shouldn't be talking to me. But instead I replied: "Yes, it was very hard. His death really hurt me."

"Why don't you join the troupe and express your pain through theater?" Victor said. "We're all good people." His hand swooped in a circle to encompass the actors, who sat on the ground talking to each other in hushed tones.

"I'll try," I said, not knowing where my answer came from. "I'll try."

Victor created a role for me in the HIV/AIDS play as a villager mourning the woman who had died. All I had to do was cry. It was a small part, but I found I liked it. We ran through the skit a couple more times before Victor called it quits.

I thanked Mariatu, waved goodbye to Victor, and went back to my tent. I didn't feel happy, but some of the heaviness inside of me had started to lift. Victor was right: pretending to cry onstage did offer some relief from my pain.

The next Sunday, I returned to the theater troupe. I didn't tell anyone in my family where I was going, just that I would be back later. "Don't worry about me," I yelled.

The following weekend, I went out to the theater troupe again. After we'd run through the skit a few times, we danced and sang. Some of the boys brought out drums. Even though they had no hands, they could still drum like nothing had happened to them. I found myself swaying to the music and singing the chorus of some popular Temne songs.

By the time we were done, it was dinnertime. Victor walked with me back through the camp. On the way, we passed by his tent. His wife had prepared a plate of rice and vegetables, and Victor invited me to eat with him.

"I was raped," I whispered halfway through the meal.

"I know," was his reply.

"Should I get tested for HIV/AIDS?"

"Yes, Mariatu," he said. "Yes."

I was shaking as the nurse at the camp pinched me with a needle and then filled a vial with my blood. It seemed anything good that happened to me was immediately followed by something bad, so I worried that maybe I was HIV-positive. I was cursed, and part of me felt it was for a good reason: I had killed Abdul by not loving him, so I deserved my fate.

My thoughts drifted to a woman in the camp who Victor said was suffering from AIDS. Her once-robust body had shrunk to half its size. Her eyes were sunken, and her face and arms were covered in open sores. Initially the woman had gone for walks around the camp using a stick for a cane. Now she spent most of her days lying on a straw mat outside her tent, covered in a thin blanket, moaning. I passed by her on my way to the theater troupe.

I closed my eyes and prayed, just as I had done the night of the rebel attack: "Allah, I know I was a bad mother. I know I didn't deserve sweet little Abdul, and that's why you took him from me. But please don't let me have this virus. Please! I don't want to die slowly like this woman at the camp. You kept me alive after Manarma for some reason. I promise, from now on for the rest of my life, I will try to think positively and be a good person if you spare me from this virus."

For the next few weeks, I was on pins and needles waiting for the test results. I tried to be a good person, as I had promised. Whenever Adamsay, Fatmata, Abibatu, or Marie talked to me, I made every effort to be attentive. I'd help the women cook dinner, fetching rice from the market, stirring the cassava leaves. I even ground some rice and cassava, though my arms kept slipping as I heaved the pole up and down into the gourd. At dinnertime, I would give my stone to Adamsay or one of my other cousins to sit on, while I crossed my legs and sat on the ground. We'd always eaten from one big plate, but now I waited for Adamsay and the others to finish before I ate. I used a big silver spoon that attached to my arms with velcro.

"What's going on with you?" Mohamed asked one night.

"Usually you're the first one gobbling up all the food!" Ibrahim added with his crooked smile.

"Ah, Mariatu," Mohamed continued. "You must want something from us. Perhaps to meet Sorie." Ibrahim and Mohamed had befriended Sorie, a boy from the camp, shortly after his arrival a few months earlier. Sorie was lean and fit, with a big wide smile, much like Mohamed's.

"No," I replied calmly. "I don't want to be with a boy ever again. I've had enough of them. But you were all so kind to me when Abdul was here that I want to help out as much as I can

117

from now on."

Mohamed and Ibrahim got up, helped each other wash the bottoms of their arms with water from a plastic kettle, and then pounced on me, knocking me to the ground. Mohamed tousled my hair while Ibrahim tickled my stomach.

"I love these boys so much," I thought when they had pulled me back up into a sitting position. I watched as they ran together down the aisle of sky blue tents, punching each other playfully in the stomach and shoulders. They were off to kick a soccer ball around with some other boys at an empty housing lot not far from the camp.

After they had disappeared from view, I lay down on my back and looked up at the big fluffy clouds. "When I die, I want it to be quick," I thought, "not drawn-out and painful.

"Salieu," I pledged, "if you are listening and watching like you said you would, I want you to know that I plan on having a long life. A long and very good life, in which I start doing good things to help people."

When I went back to see the nurse, I had to wait outside in a long line. After about two hours, I made it inside the building, where I sat down on an examination table. The nurse was reading from a clipboard as she approached me.

"Mariatu," she said with a smile. "You tested negative. You do not have HIV/AIDS."

"Maybe," I thought as I walked back to my tent, "my luck is finally changing."

Every Saturday and Sunday from then on, I joined the theater troupe in the center of the camp. In addition to the play on HIV/AIDS, we worked on a new skit about forgiveness and reconciliation. We re-enacted a scene from the war in which some of the youth played victims while others played the boy soldiers. As in the play I had seen when Mariatu introduced me to the troupe, the boy rebels pretended to cut off their victims' hands and then to burn down the village. But the last part of this play was different.

In one scene, a man played the head commando of the rebels, ordering the boy rebels around. "You need to be fighters! You need to kill!" he yelled. "Take this to make you strong men," he said, handing the boys drugs.

One boy rebel said no, so the commando beat him.

In the second-to-last scene, the boy rebels huddled together, crying. They admitted their crimes to one another and wished they could return to their own villages and their old lives—much like all of us at Aberdeen were wishing we could do.

The final scene had the boy rebels and the victims walking out onstage, arm in arm, and singing about peace.

As I sat on the ground and watched, I realized that the boy rebels who had hurt me must have families somewhere. I thought back to the rebel who'd said he wanted me to join them in the bush. "Would he have asked me to kill?" I wondered.

Mariatu broke into my thoughts. Linking her arm through mine, she pulled me to my feet and then dragged me up onstage. "It's time to dance," she sang out.

The boys started drumming, just like boys did back in Magborou. Two girls at a time came forward and did a dance duet. The rest of us sang and swayed to the rhythm and beat.

When it was my turn to be in the center, I closed my eyes.

119

My knees bent. My torso moved down toward the ground and up again, then side to side. I repeated the pattern, immersing myself in the music. I felt really alive for the first time in ages.

One Sunday, just as we ended our practice for the day, Victor motioned for us to be quiet.

"I have something to tell you," he said. He paused, keeping us in suspense.

"Come on, Victor. Spit it out," Mariatu implored.

"We're going to perform in public," he announced, his eyes bright.

"Oh, that's all," Mariatu said, rolling her eyes. "Who's visiting the camp this time?" Whenever aid agency officials or a politician came to the camp, the theater troupe performed— just as I had been asked to perform for the media when Abdul was alive. When I told my story, journalists furiously wrote down my answers in tiny books. The theater troupe also told stories, through skits, dances, and songs.

"No," Victor replied, winking at Mariatu. "We've been asked to perform at Brookfields Stadium in a couple of weeks' time for a whole bunch of people, including some government ministers."

My chest constricted. "I can't perform in front of other people," I declared. Brookfields was the largest place for people to meet in all of Freetown.

"Yes, you can," Victor admonished. "You all can, and you all will. We will do such a good job that the war will end and peace will come again to Sierra Leone!"

"Don't get your hopes up," Mariatu moaned.

I moaned too, for a different reason. I was trying to think of the best excuse I could offer to get out of performing. But something else in me was just as strong, and I decided to join the theater troupe onstage after all. We had an important purpose: to help raise awareness of my country's problems.

CHAPTER 13

"Mariatu! Mariatu!" Mohamed called out.

I was walking back from the clock tower, tired and dusty after a day of begging. All I wanted was some rice and sauce, some vegetables if Abibatu and Marie had prepared any, and then bed. I went to sleep early now most nights, in preparation for our performance at the soccer stadium. I was still worried I would make a fool of myself, but Mariatu was so thrilled about the event that I didn't want to rain on her parade. Sometimes she got so excited she started jumping up and down, squealing in delight. Her enthusiasm was catching, and we'd jump facing each other, going faster and faster. Our hysteria turned into a game in which we'd see who could jump the highest.

"Some fancy lady wants to see you," Mohamed gasped, running up to me. Mohamed's baby fat had disappeared since we'd moved to the camp, and he was growing into a handsome man, with a big white smile that could charm anyone. "Hurry," he urged, hopping from foot to foot. "She's at the tent. She's at the tent. I think it's your time."

Adamsay was leaving for Germany in less than a month. About six young people from the camp had moved to the United States, and several others were on a relocation list. But so far no one had shown any interest in me.

"Mohamed, you're such a jokester," I called as we wove in and out of the market stalls, jumping over plastic laundry tubs, boxes, dogs, and cats. "Don't get my hopes up!"

"Mariatu, I'm not lying. She's real. The woman is real. She's there at the camp, talking to Marie and Abibatu and asking for you."

My heart leapt. What if Mohamed was right? What if I could leave this place full of so much sadness, end my days of feeling worthless because I had to beg richer Sierra Leoneans for handouts? Abdul still entered my dreams at night. When I passed other babies at the camp, slung on their mothers' backs, I'd look away and quicken my pace. Moving to a foreign place might be a remedy for the guilt that still plagued me.

Mohamed and I took as many shortcuts as we knew, down alleyways, behind and around other people's tents. En route, someone shouted: "What's your hurry? It's not like you're going anywhere."

I wanted to shout back at him, "Yes I am! I'm going to the United States!"

When we got to our tent, Marie was lighting the fire. Standing beside her was a woman wearing a straight brown skirt and a white blouse. She was the same height as Marie but wider, with short curly hair.

"Hello," the woman said when I stopped in front of her. "I'm Comfort. Are you Mariatu?"

"Yes," I panted, still breathless from our run.

"Well, then. If you are Mariatu Kamara, I have a message for you."

"What is it?"

"If you come to my office tomorrow morning, I will give you the message, and we can talk more about things then." She gave me directions to her office, then went on her way.

I stood pondering the possibilities. Would I really be going to this place called the United States, which people said was the best place in the world to live?

I could have slept in the next morning, but I got up with Adamsay. After my cousins left, I changed into my best clothes, a red Africana docket-and-lappa. I washed my only shoes, a pair of orange flip-flops, and then set off.

Comfort's office wasn't far from the camp. I had never been in an office building before. The closest I'd ever got to those official-looking places was standing at their gates with Adamsay, asking business people for money on their way home from work. Usually one of the security guards would order us to get lost.

As I walked toward the front door that morning, I half-expected the security guard to shoo me away. But he didn't. He smiled and opened the door for me instead.

I found the staircase at the end of the hall, right where Comfort had told me it would be, and counted out the four flights to her floor. When I reached the landing, she was there to meet me. "Perfect timing," she said with approval.

Today Comfort was wearing a blue Africana docket-and-lappa, with some big brown beads. "You look very nice," I complimented her.

"Thank you," she said. "I like to wear both Western clothes and Africana outfits."

Comfort's office was a big room full of bookshelves. Posters of flowers and framed certificates and diplomas hung on the walls. When Comfort saw me looking at them, she explained that she was a social worker. She helped people at the amputee camp with non-medical problems, such as reuniting with their families. "Some families are very ashamed of their members who have lost limbs from the war," she said. "At first they don't want anything to do with these people who are disabled. I help the families accept their loved ones."

I wondered a little at what she said. Until the day before, I had never seen Comfort at the camp, and my family got along just fine. They didn't view me any differently than they had before the attack. They still bossed me around: "Go get some water, Mariatu! Go buy some peppers! Go brush your teeth!" I wasn't exactly sure whom Comfort was helping. But I didn't ask.

Comfort motioned me to a chair beside her desk.

"A man phoned from Canada," she said, sitting down across from me. "His name is Bill, and he wants to find the girl he read about in a newspaper article." Comfort reached over and handed me a newspaper clipping. To my surprise, it showed a photograph of me, holding Abdul. "Is this you?"

"Yes," I said quietly, staring into the face of my little son. "That's me." I had to blink back my tears.

Comfort didn't seem to notice my distress. "If you are the person in the photograph, this man Bill wants to help you. His family read your story, and they would like to give you money for food and clothes."

"What is Canada?" I asked.

Comfort pulled a big book she called an atlas out from

behind her desk. "This is North America," she said, running her hand over one of the pages. "Canada is a country that sits above the United States."

"Oh," I said. "Is Canada safe?"

"Yes, it's safe there. And it's a rich country. It's also very cold. For half the year, it snows."

I had never heard this word *snow*. Comfort explained that it was like white salt that falls from the sky when it is very chilly. I pictured in my head a cool Sierra Leone night in spring, with white salt falling all around me.

"It's colder than the coldest night here!" Comfort said, as if she could read my mind. "Don't compare it to any day or night you've felt in Sierra Leone."

"So, this man Bill, is he taking me to Canada?" I asked.

"No. But if you pray for it, maybe he will."

I told Marie and Alie about Bill when I got back to the camp. They were happy for me, and also for themselves. They talked about all the food they would buy when this man's money started coming in.

"But I want to go to Canada," I said. "I want him to bring me to this place."

"We'll get some fruit, pineapple and coconut," Alie continued, ignoring me. "We haven't tasted such sweetness in a long time!"

Marie and Alie also mentioned the new houses a nonprofit group from Norway was building for amputees. Alie said we would qualify for the program, because four of us in the family were amputees and we didn't have a home. The rebels had destroyed most of Magborou, including Marie and Alie's hut.

"Money from Bill," Alie continued, "will help us in the move to the new house."

"You've done really well," Marie exclaimed, patting me on the back.

I left Marie and Alie still talking about Bill, and headed straight to the camp mosque. A few men were praying in the men's section at the front of the large blue tent. I was the only female in our section at the back. I knelt. I put my head on the floor, and I whispered over and over again: "Thank you, Allah."

A week later, I was back in Comfort's office. I sat nervously on the other side of her desk, waiting for Bill to call on the telephone. I was scared that maybe he wouldn't like me. I didn't speak English, and I worried he would move on to another girl who could communicate with him better. A few girls at the camp had been to school and learned some words of English there.

I knew what a telephone was from the medical clinic in Port Loko. There was only one doctor on staff at the clinic, treating more than a hundred patients a day, so the nurses often used a telephone to call Freetown, seeking advice from the doctors there. But I'd never seen a telephone. We didn't have them in our village. We didn't have electricity in our village either, or even a generator. Many people in Freetown used generators when the electricity was out, which happened frequently because of the war.

After a few minutes we heard a ringing sound. "Here he is," Comfort said, picking up the top part of the telephone.

Comfort talked to Bill for a while. Then she cupped the telephone receiver in her hands and spoke to me. "Bill doesn't speak Temne or Krio, so you won't understand each other, but at least you can hear what he sounds like." She held the phone up to my ear.

"Hello," I said in Krio.

"CHA CHA … CHOO CHOO CHOOO," Bill replied. At least, that's what his English sounded like to me.

"My name is Mariatu. Thank you for helping me. I am very grateful," I said in Temne.

Comfort took the phone back. While she continued her conversation with Bill in English, I looked around the room at the diplomas and certificates. I had seen similar framed papers in the hospital in Freetown. The diplomas said that so-and-so had completed her training, the nurses told me. I had asked one nurse what school was like. "Sometimes it's very difficult," she said. "But going to school opens new worlds for girls. When you go to school, you can do important things and help other people. You don't have to stay in your village and have baby after baby."

I'd thought at the time: "I'd like to go to school one day."

Comfort hung up the telephone and gazed over at me. "Bill says he's putting a box of clothes in the mail for you, and some money. It should be here in a month. I'll come and get you when the package arrives."

The next few weeks were a whirlwind. I eagerly awaited my package from Bill.

At the same time, we were practicing for our performance at the soccer stadium. The theater troupe now met not only on the weekends but also a few nights each week. Often we ended our rehearsal early to make posters announcing the event.

Those who knew how to write and draw designed the posters. The rest of us helped distribute them throughout Freetown.

Victor had given me a line in the HIV/AIDS skit. "Yes, she was such a good woman," I was to say about the lady who had died from the virus. I was scheduled to be onstage several other times to dance and sing.

The morning of our performance, Victor handed out costumes that his wife and some of the other women at the camp had sewn for us. For the HIV/AIDS scene, I would put on an orange Africana outfit. I'd wear a skirt made from rice bags cut into strips when I danced and sang.

I was more nervous that day than I had ever been. Victor had hired some minibuses to take us to the stadium, and we gathered in the main section of the camp about an hour before.

"Are you scared?" Mariatu asked me. We'd folded our costumes into the same black plastic bags we used while begging.

"Yes," I replied. "What if I trip and fall off the stage?"

"If you don't fall on your own," Mariatu teased, "I'll push you off."

"You be careful," I teased back, "because I plan on pushing you off before you get to me."

We laughed at the picture of the two of us brawling onstage. "That's exactly what the government will want to show the foreign nonprofit people," Mariatu chuckled. "Two girls wrestling each other!"

Victor interrupted our giggles. Posters had been tacked on bulletin boards, the sides of buildings, and gates all over town, and he'd heard that about a thousand people were expected to attend our performance, including the heads of the charities that helped us at the camp.

My fear that I would humiliate myself crept in again.

"Victor," I said, pulling him aside. "You should go ahead without me. I am not of the same caliber as the others, who know how to act, sing, and dance."

I could hear the minibuses approaching, and I was hoping he'd say there wasn't room for me after all. Instead, he reassured me. "I'm very proud of you, Mariatu. You've come a long way with your healing. You've suffered so much, and look at what you're doing now—about to go onstage and perform."

"But aren't you afraid I'll make the theater troupe look silly?"

"No," Victor responded. "Quite the opposite. We are doing really good work here, through theater, to help the amputees. Having you onstage will help the charities see how important theater is and get them to support theater programs in other parts of the country. Besides," he said, tenderly rubbing my shoulder, "we can't go on unless you are with us. We are a group, a family, and we won't be separated because you're nervous. It's natural to be nervous. If you weren't, I'd think there was something still wrong with you."

I peeked out from behind the curtains once we'd arrived. Nearly every chair assembled around the stage that had been set up in the stadium was occupied. I peered at all the faces, recognizing no one, although Sulaiman and his wife, Mariatu, had promised to be somewhere in the crowd. Many of the men wore suits, and some were white-skinned, like the journalists. The day was hot, so the ladies in their crisp Africana dresses were fanning themselves with the posters we had made.

Some of the boys in our group assembled themselves onstage and, with the curtain still drawn, began to drum. That was the sign that we were about to begin. The first part of the performance involved us all being onstage, singing a song about the war that Victor and the troupe had written. Because I was short, I'd be in the front row.

Victor pulled the curtains back. Just as it was my turn to go onstage, I hesitated. But Mariatu, right behind me, gave me a shove. The bright spotlights startled me for a moment. I must have looked like a wide-eyed deer. Somehow I managed to find my spot, though, and I began singing along with the rest of the group. I soon forgot I was up in front of all those strangers. We sang and danced just like we had done in practice back at the camp.

I said my line and wept in the HIV/AIDS play. We got a standing ovation for our skit on forgiveness and reconciliation. The event ended with us all together onstage again, arm in arm.

Sulaiman and Mariatu found me after the performance. I was giggling with Mariatu and a girl named Memunatu, who had lost one hand during the Freetown invasion.

Sulaiman gave me a big hug. "I am so proud of you," he said, wiping a tear from his eye. "I'm going to miss you when you move to this place called Canada!"

"Don't worry, Sulaiman," I said. "I'm not moving any-where."

How wrong I was.

CHAPTER 14

"So, what do you think about going to England?" the young woman in front of me asked. Yabom was her name, she'd informed us.

"I don't know," I mumbled. "Do I have to give you an answer right away?"

Marie glared at me. *Wrong answer.* We had been talking a lot in the evenings about the prospect of my moving to Canada, and about how moving away would be the best thing for me and for the family financially. The youth who had gone to other countries sent their families as much as 300,000 leones, or $100, a month and mailed them items we'd never heard of, like chocolates. Now, out of nowhere, another woman who'd shown up at the camp was offering me England instead.

"All right," I said as enthusiastically as I could. "England sounds great." I did want out of the camp, badly, but Adamsay's program in Germany had fallen through, and I wanted her to leave before me. Adamsay was always doing nice things for me, like holding me in her arms when I had a bad dream at night. She deserved it.

"We'll start organizing the paperwork tomorrow," Yabom

replied. "You need a birth certificate and a passport."

"But she doesn't have any of these things," Marie jumped in to say.

"I know," said the woman. "I'll help Mariatu apply for her papers."

"Fine," I said, forcing a smile. "I'll do whatever you want."

We'd been living at the camp for close to two years now. Marie, Abibatu, and Fatmata's days were almost always the same. They'd sit around talking to each other and waiting for my cousins and me to return from begging with money or food we had bought at the market. The women, including Fatmata (who, with Abdul, was now living at the camp full-time), did the cooking. Marie, more than anyone, longed to return to a village, any village. Like Mabinty, she needed something active to do. Marie and Alie had high hopes we'd get one of the houses under construction for the amputees, and they knew they'd need money to make the move.

About four months had passed since Bill and I had talked on the telephone. He had sent a package with some Western-style clothing, including T-shirts and pants two sizes too big for me, and about 150,000 leones ($50). According to Comfort, he'd promised that another package was on the way. But he had never indicated that he wanted to bring me to Canada, which upset Marie and Alie.

"It's too bad what happened to you," Marie had said. "But you must see the positive in everything. Right now the positive for you is finding someone in a foreign country who will take you in and give you the education you need to get a job; and for you to be able to send us, your family, money when you have it."

133

I wanted to make Marie happy. I wanted to do the right thing.

Yabom said she was a social worker, like Comfort, though I'd never seen her at the camp either. Her initial approach had been a lot like Comfort's. "There is this man," she said. More than anyone I had met so far, Yabom talked with her hands. They flew through the air, accentuating her every word. I followed her hands for a while, then focused on her shiny, smooth skin and big round eyes. "This man lives in England, and he has raised money to pay for your flight to London so you can have some medical treatment."

"What kind of medical treatment?"

"Well, this man, David, wants you to go to a hospital where the nurses and doctors help people who have lost limbs in car crashes or farming accidents," explained Yabom. "He wants the hospital to fit you with prosthetic hands, which he will pay for. Do you know what prosthetic hands are?"

"No," I replied. The word meant nothing to me.

"Well," Yabom continued, searching for the words, "David wants to give you ... how should I explain this ... fake hands. They are hands you can use just like real hands, to eat and write, do all the things you used to do."

Fake hands? I couldn't picture it. A few kids in the camp who'd had parts of their legs chopped off by the rebels had fake legs. They attached these wooden contraptions, like big logs, to the remaining part of their leg with long pieces of tape. But the logs always seemed to be falling off. The kids actually got around better when they hopped on one leg than when they tried walking with two. I couldn't imagine wooden hands and fingers being of any help. But for my family's sake, I knew I had to give it a try.

On our first day together, Yabom took me to one of the government offices near the presidential building. As we stepped inside the front gates, I stopped to look at the Sierra Leonean flag flying on a tall pole. Our flag is simple: blue, green, and white stripes. I had only seen the flag a couple of times before, always in Freetown.

"Do you know the history of Sierra Leone?" Yabom asked as we stood side by side, gazing up at the flag.

"No," I replied. "I don't know much at all, just what I've heard about the war at the camp."

"Well, then," she said, leading me to a bench at the side of the building.

It was quiet inside the front gates, not busy and noisy like the street outside. Birds were chirping, a sound I had not heard since Magborou. Usually their songs were drowned out by Freetown's constantly honking minibus and car horns and the chatter of many, many people.

"Back in the 1500s, a Portuguese explorer was sailing the West African coast," Yabom began. "When he reached what we call Freetown today, it was storming. The thunder echoed against the mountains, and the sailor thought the noise sounded like roaring lions. He named the area Sierra Lyoa, or Mountain Lion."

She glanced up at the flag. "For much of our modern history, Sierra Leone belonged to other people. We were a colony of England, where you are about to go, which means that the

British, or the English, said Sierra Leone belonged to them."

The British had built homes in Sierra Leone and mined the country's resources, Yabom explained. They had tried to modernize Sierra Leone and make the country run like a modern European nation.

"What happened?" I questioned.

"It's complicated," she replied, pausing to search for the words. "You see, Europeans saw Sierra Leoneans, as well as other African people, as a source of, well … as slaves."

Yabom described how, in the slave trade, people from Africa were forced onto ships and sent to North America to work for free. "Many people died on these ships, and those who survived endured long hours of terribly hard work and separation from their families. Babies were taken from their mothers. Husbands and wives were torn apart. When slavery started to be condemned, many of the freed slaves returned to Freetown. That's why the city is named as it is. These former slaves were from not only Sierra Leone but all over Africa. They didn't speak Temne or Mende. They spoke Krio, which is a broken form of the English they had learned in the West."

Yabom put her arm around me. "My dear, Sierra Leone only gained its independence from the British in the 1960s. That's likely just before your mother was born. Sierra Leone became a recognized country ten years after that. There was much corruption among government officials. Look around you," she said, waving her hands in the air. "We are a rich country, full of resources, from diamonds to bauxite. But we're also very, very poor. Money from the sale of our resources doesn't reach the average person. Liberia, which borders Sierra Leone to the east, was already engaged in a civil war when war broke out here. A man named Foday Sankoh launched the Revolutionary United Front from Liberia in 1991, when you were only four or five. Sankoh said his goal was to end the abuse of power by Sierra Leone politicians. He felt they were stealing the money they made from selling our resources abroad. But Sankoh was worse than any of the politicians he accused of thievery. You know the old saying, when you point a finger at someone, there are probably three fingers pointing back at you?"

I nodded. Marie often used a version of this expression to discourage us from telling on one another for things like taking too much food. "Child," she'd say to the boy or girl who had lodged the complaint, "if you're accusing someone of doing something bad, you're probably thinking of doing it yourself."

"Sankoh should have looked at his own fingers," Yabom said. "He started mining the diamonds, trading them in Liberia for weapons to fuel the war. He encouraged boys to become soldiers. These boys had broken spirits by the time Sankoh got to them. Sierra Leone is so poor that, without schools and jobs, there were few things for these boys to look forward to. So they were easy prey for him. Mariatu, we are one of the poorest countries in the world. You will see soon enough when you move to England. You'll see the Londoners' clothes, their expensive houses, the food they eat, their theaters and museums. We have our beautiful sandy beaches, but that's about all Freetown has that England doesn't."

We sat outside talking for about an hour. The Sierra Leone flag stopped flapping when the warm morning wind died.

"We must go inside and fill out your paperwork," Yabom

said, looking at the position of the sun. "It's early afternoon, and if we don't get this done, you're not moving anywhere!"

I had to answer a bunch of questions before the government could process my birth certificate. In a first-floor office, Yabom and I had been seated across from a woman who wore the uniform I now identified with business: a white blouse and a straight beige skirt with high-heeled black shoes.

The first few questions were easy. "Where were you born? Where do you live now? What is your mother's full name?" the woman asked me.

Then, "What is your date of birth?"

That question stumped me. I looked first at the woman, then at Yabom. "I don't know," I shrugged.

"You're not alone," the woman said. "In most parts of Sierra Leone, children's birthdates are not recorded. But we have to put down something. Can we take a guess?"

"What time of year do you think you were born?" Yabom asked me.

I thought long and hard. "My father told me it rained the day I was born. But the way he told the story, it sounded like it wasn't supposed to rain quite yet. So maybe at the end of the dry season?" I speculated.

"Let's write May," Yabom said. The woman scribbled down the month.

"Do you have a favorite number?" the woman asked next. "We need to write down an actual day in May."

I'd only learned about numbers once I moved to Freetown and started begging. I'd discovered then that leones come in many denominations. "I don't know. I like twenty-five," I said.

"May 25 it is, then," said the woman.

Even though I'd never celebrated a birthday, I knew I'd been alive for 14 years. So May 25, 1986, became my official date of birth.

At the end of the questions, the government official said she needed me to sign my name.

"I don't know how to write," I told her.

"The government requires official documents, like your birth certificate and passport, to have a signature. Since so many people have lost their hands in the war, it's permissible to sign with your feet. So we will take a toe imprint."

Yabom bent over and slipped off my right flip-flop. She cleaned my big toe with a dry towel, then squished it into some blue ink. She pressed my inky toe down on several different papers.

"Good," the woman said when we were done. "You should have your birth certificate in about six weeks."

"And that will be six weeks closer to the time you leave for England," Yabom said to me as we got up to leave.

Many times since we'd met, I'd decided to tell Yabom about Bill. But I'd always had seconds thoughts. It wasn't that I didn't trust Yabom. Quite the contrary: her soft manners reminded me of Fatmata, who did so much for me but never asked once for anything in return. I worried, though, that the trip to England might not happen if I told Yabom some other Western man was interested in me too.

The women in my family had started to collect Western-style clothes for me. I'm very tiny; when I came to live in North

America, I learned that I am about a size four. Since most of the clothes donated to the camp were larger, Fatmata and Abibatu solicited Father Maurizio's help. Soon afterwards, he passed along some Italian-style jeans, which were slim-fitting and hugged my body like a bathing suit. The T-shirts he'd found were snug too.

When I first tried on a pair of jeans, I shrieked. "How can women walk in these!" I exclaimed. I couldn't even bend my knees.

Fatmata laughed. "You can see every bend and curve of your body."

Soon there was barely room to turn around in the tent. The walls of our rooms were already lined with our spare clothes, pots and pans, bags of rice, and other food supplies we'd set aside to last us through the rainy season. Added to that was a big black suitcase Yabom had bought me. I packed the clothes from Father Maurizio inside.

One night Marie, Abibatu, Fatmata, Adamsay, and I sat alone by the fire. The men and boys were at the mosque. Usually when we women were together, we'd all talk at once. But that night everyone was quiet.

"Mariatu," Marie said, poking the fire with a stick, "I am sorry I didn't listen to you that day you had the bad dream about palm oil."

Her apology surprised me, and I didn't know what to say.

"None of us may ever see our homes again," Abibatu commented. "This war, it's been going on too long, with too much suffering. But you, Mariatu, you have a chance. You have a chance to make something of yourself."

"I wish I could go," Adamsay said in a small voice. Her face was covered in tears. I wanted to fold her into my arms and say to her: "You go instead."

"You remember how, after Manarma, it took me a week to find my way out of the bush?" she said.

I nodded slowly. By the time Adamsay got to the Port Loko medical clinic, the flesh around her wounds had rotted and was full of gangrene. Doctors had to finish what the rebels had started by cutting off a large portion of her left arm.

"You're smarter than me, Mariatu," Adamsay went on. "You've always had a sense of direction, and you are good at figuring out people's motives. Will you use your mind for me, get very smart in this place called England, and show me how to find my way?"

"You're our hope for the future, Mariatu," Marie said. "Take that medical treatment, go to school, and get a job."

No one spoke for a minute. Sparks from the fire rose into the air.

Marie broke the silence. "Don't look back, Mariatu. If you look back, you will live your life with regrets and what-could-have-beens. Always look forward."

My family, along with Victor and some members of the theater troupe, gathered to see me off the morning I left for England. I missed Mariatu. She had moved to the United States shortly after our performance at the soccer stadium.

"Don't forget about us," said Victor when it was his turn to say farewell.

"How could I ever forget you?" I protested. And it was true.

I knew I would never forget him or anyone in the theater troupe. Memunatu and the others sang a goodbye song, and I danced along with them.

Mohamed was the first to come forward from my family.

"Goodbye, Mariatu," he said, embracing me with his big, bulging-muscle arms.

I tried really hard not to cry as Abibatu pushed a covered tin plate of rice and sauce into my arms. "For the ferry," she said tearfully. "You might get hungry."

"Come, Mariatu," Marie said, picking up my suitcase. Marie is even tinier than I am, and seeing her lugging my big suitcase made me laugh.

"Help her," I shouted to Ibrahim and Mohamed.

"Ah, Mariatu," Ibrahim exclaimed with a smile as he and Mohamed each took a side of the suitcase and lifted it onto their heads. "I sure won't miss you bossing us around!"

I giggled, pushing my body into his in an attempt to knock him down. I gave up and kissed the boys on their cheeks instead.

Everyone accompanied me to the taxi-minibus waiting on the street. Yabom was already inside.

When my suitcase was safely stored in the trunk of the bus, and I was sitting in the front seat beside the driver, I leaned out and waved. My family and friends were smiling up at me.

I kept smiling even though I was shaking inside. I felt a great weight land on my shoulders. "Will I ever see any of you again?" I thought as the minibus pulled away. "Can I ever live up to what you want from me?"

I blinked back my tears. As we continued along the dusty road, I remembered Marie's words: "Always look forward."

CHAPTER 15

"Another rainy day," I growled as I rolled out of bed, rubbing my eyes.

From the kitchen window, I peered at the choppy Thames River below. "There's more rain in London than I ever saw during the rainy season in Sierra Leone," I said to Yabom, who was sipping a cup of coffee. "Do we have to go out today?"

"We should try to do something," Yabom replied. A piece of paper taped to the refrigerator listed all the places David had recommended we visit. "Maybe the Natural History Museum?"

We'd been in London two weeks, and it had rained every day. We weren't scheduled to be at the hospital yet, so David suggested we settle in by exploring the city. Also on his list were the Houses of Parliament, which included a big clock called Big Ben, Westminster Abbey, St. Paul's Cathedral, and Madame Tussauds.

"What is Madame Tussauds?" I asked Yabom.

"David says it features lifelike mannequins of all our favorite celebrities."

"What's a celebrity?" I asked.

"I have no idea," replied Yabom, shaking her head.

The two-bedroom apartment where we were living belonged to Mariama, the Sierra Leonean woman who had helped David organize my trip. Yabom turned on the television for me, and I sat cross-legged watching a band called 'N Sync perform. I didn't understand a word they were singing, though, and I couldn't get into the rhythm.

"This Western music doesn't have a real beat to it," I called out to Yabom, who was washing our breakfast dishes. "Where are the drummers?"

I turned off the television as Mariama had shown me and joined Yabom in the kitchen. "I don't like this country," I said. "It's always gray. In Sierra Leone everything is colorful: the clothes people wear, the trees, and the flowers."

"You'll get used to London," she replied. "It will take a while to see how things work in England, and to appreciate the different colors here."

"Gray is hard to appreciate," I laughed.

Everyone on the London streets walked quickly, never seeming to look at each other or say hello. They'd push past without even a nod. Whenever we left Mariama's apartment, we had to put on strange boots called Wellingtons and uncomfortable rubber coats.

Yabom coaxed me into an outing, and I wrapped my arms tightly around myself as my teeth began to chatter. London was not only rainy but chilly. "Yabom," I said, "can we go inside somewhere?"

"Let's go for a ride on the bus," she said.

"Yes!" I exclaimed. "Can we sit on the top?"

The first time I'd laid eyes on the red double-decker buses,

I told Yabom we had to go for a ride. The poda-podas in Sierra Leone seat maybe 15 people, with another 10 bodies sitting on the floor and hanging off the sides and back. I couldn't even count the number of people these buses held.

Mariama had moved to England before the war, and she was very active in London's Sierra Leonean community, organizing dinners and assisting new immigrants to find housing and jobs. She'd helped raise the money for my medical treatment mostly from other Sierra Leoneans living in the city.

"We started to read about the amputees in the newspaper," Mariama told me, "and we just had to do something."

I had my own bedroom in Mariama's apartment, something I'd never had back home. The room was dark, though, since the window faced out onto another gray apartment building, and I didn't like sleeping alone. The room felt big and hollow with just me inside it. I was used to sleeping with someone on both sides of me. At night, I'd felt safe listening to their breathing. In my London bedroom, all I could hear in the dead of night was the hum of the refrigerator and the electric wires.

Since we'd arrived in England, I'd started to have bad dreams about the rebels. I dreamt that they were chasing me. I dreamt that I was walking along the clay dirt road to Port Loko all over again. A hawk was calling out to me, telling me danger was on the horizon. When I looked over into the tall elephant grasses, I could see the main rebel man. He raised his hand and ordered the boys to attack, and that's when I saw their faces again. Their eyes were wild, their cheeks were all puffed out, and they were covered in blood—my blood. The boys yelled as they rushed out of the bush toward me. Before I knew it, they were on top of me, swinging their machetes.

I'd wake up from these nightmares screaming. Yabom would come running from the bedroom she shared with Mariama next door, her hair sticking up, her nightdress rumpled. She'd get under the covers beside me and stroke my hair the way Fatmata and Abibatu had when I was in the hospital. I'd fall back asleep only to have more dreams.

"Maybe you're having these dreams now," Yabom told me one night, "because you feel far away and safe from the rebels now. Maybe emotional things are coming up for you, memories that you need to talk about."

"I've never really talked about the attack," I said to her. "The only people I spoke to were the doctors and the journalists. All of them were so busy writing things down that they barely looked at me. Half the time, I didn't even know if they were listening."

"Why don't you tell me, then?" Yabom said softly, rolling onto her side. I liked the way she smelled, like Ivory soap, and her body felt so warm beside me. She held me as I let my life story unravel. I told her about Magborou, and about how I had come to live with Marie and Alie. I shared what I remembered about the rebels, and about the man I met in the bush who helped me find the road to Port Loko. I even told her about Salieu, and about the guilt I felt that Adamsay wasn't the one chosen to leave.

"She deserves it more than me," I sighed. "She's such a good person, and I'm rotten. I killed Abdul."

Yabom listened as few people had ever listened to me

before. When I paused, she told me things about her own life. Yabom was married and wanted to have children of her own, but not until the war ended. "When it's safe, so my son or daughter has a chance," she said. "Do you still want children one day?"

"Yes," I told her. "I always wanted four children, and I think I still do."

"You know, Abdul didn't die because of you," she said gently. "Lots of babies die in Sierra Leone from diseases and malnutrition. You were just a baby, and babies aren't supposed to be having babies. Besides, it sounds like Abdul had lots of love from Marie, Abibatu, Fatmata, and Mabinty. Just like you when you came to live with Marie and Alie. Did you ever think for a moment it was because your mother didn't love you?"

"No," I said. I had never thought of it that way.

I was scared, I confided to Yabom. "My family wants me to go to school and get a good job, but how can I do that with no hands? I want so much for them to be proud of me. I want so much for Alie, Marie, and the others to go back to Magborou and their old lives. They can't even pay for transportation to move there. I want to do well and raise the money to help them return. I just don't know how I am going to do that."

Yabom propped herself up on her elbow. "You have so much riding on your shoulders," she said. "If you get your new hands, and eventually an education, you can get a job one day. Then your family won't have to worry about feeding you or looking after you. That's all you need to think about now— becoming independent. Don't worry about the others yet."

"All right," I said, although I didn't feel any better about the subject. "I will try."

The electric alarm clock on my dresser said it was nearly four in the morning. We'd talked almost all night. "Let's go buy some flowers today, and then you can start learning your ABCs," Yabom suggested. "We'll brighten up your room and your spirits."

With those words, both of us drifted off to sleep.

Yabom had said it would take a while to get used to London, and David said the same thing about the prosthetic hand device. He was with Yabom, Mariama, and me in the doctor's office the first time I struggled to put it on. The contraption, made of thick leather strips and shiny silver metal, had to be strapped on like a backpack. The device was bulky and very, very heavy. I had to strain every muscle in my back and arms to get into it.

The device was only temporary, the adults tried to reassure me. My *real* fake hands, the reason I'd come to London, would take another few weeks to be made. I'd been fitted for them by having my arms placed in all sorts of plastic, gooey moulds. The new hands, I was told, would be smaller and lighter and made of plastic. Until then, I had to make do with this horrible metal device.

There was nothing I could do to make those metal hands go the way I wanted them to. Two or three times a week, the therapists at the hospital tried teaching me to pick up big plastic rings or fist-sized balls with the long, curving metal fingers. When the therapist with the straight blonde hair guided my arms, I could push a coin with the fingers from one side of a cardboard box to the other. But left on my own, I couldn't get them to go anywhere near the coin. Eventually, the weight of the fake hands would topple the box and I'd sigh with defeat and embarrassment.

"It's all right," the therapist always said in her British accent. But I could tell that even she was getting frustrated. Her creamy skin became splotchy as she tightened her fists, cheering me on like she said soccer fans do for their favorite players. I was sure the fans cheered even when they knew their favorite players weren't going to score.

David and Mariama wanted me to wear the device every day to practice. My first job in the morning, after getting changed into a pair of Father Maurizio's jeans and a long-sleeved shirt, was to put the device on by myself. I'd sit on the floor, set the device up on my bed, and slide into it that way. If it fell down, as it often did, I'd have to start all over. I tried placing it on a chair and then crawling backwards into it, but I knocked the chair over.

Yabom was sympathetic. She'd come into my room after Mariama had left for the day and help me. The first time I ate breakfast with the device on, I managed to skewer a piece of buttered toast on one of the long fingers. Yabom encouraged me to eat the toast right there and then, like meat on a stick, but I just scowled. This wasn't how I wanted to feed myself. In fact, I had become quite proficient without the device, using a spoon or a fork attached to my forearms with Velcro. I could eat anything with these utensils, from rice to teensy-weensy peas. I didn't need those fake fingers.

After the toast incident, I refused to eat breakfast. I'd come out of my bedroom with the contraption on my back and salivate just looking at the cereal boxes, cartons of milk and cream, bananas, and bread. But I'd say I wasn't hungry. I'd go back to my room and sit there moping until Yabom came and got me.

On our days off, Yabom and I explored the city. But now I hated walking in London even more. During my first weeks there, people had rushed past me; now they slowed their pace to stare at me and my metal hands. Mariama and Yabom had bought me a thick blue wool coat, two sizes too big to accommodate the metal device. My silver hands stuck out, and people would poke their faces out from under their umbrellas to see the spectacle: a tiny African girl in an oversized coat with a foot-long metal contraption poking out from each sleeve.

Before that, going to the flower shop around the corner had been my favorite pastime in London. I could spend hours smelling the pink, yellow, and red roses and white lilies and admiring the bouquets the shopkeeper made. I'd often buy gardenias with the money Mariama and David had given me for touristy things, arranging them in a glass vase on the dresser in my bedroom. Now, though, the nice saleslady with the red hair would follow me around the store in case I knocked a vase over. I had done that one day, shattering a bouquet of white roses.

As I had learned to do in Freetown while begging, I kept my eyes pointed down. But I still saw the glances from strangers. I still saw, too, the homeless people, dirty and disheveled, who used tin cans instead of black plastic shopping bags to collect donations from passersby. There was one young man who was always outside the entrance to the London Underground station near our apartment. He was maybe 20, and his blond hair was dirty and matted. He wore a torn over-coat, a knitted brown hat, and ripped, stained jeans. His hands were covered in dirt and he had yellow fingers, likely from cigarette smoking, Yabom told me. Sometimes the man would just sit on the cold cement. Sometimes he played the guitar. Once I saw him playing an African drum. He wasn't very good, not like the boys back home, whose drumming was fast and deep. But he tried.

I'd elbow Yabom as softly as I could with the contraption to indicate she should give him some money. She'd protest. "We can't be tossing our money away."

"Please, Yabom. This boy is like me back at the amputee camp," I'd plead.

Yabom would drop a few coins into the boy's guitar case. I would smile, trying to catch the boy's attention. But he too had learned not to look up.

"Why are there young people in London who have to beg?" I asked Mariama and David one night over a dinner of rice and lamb. "I thought this was a rich country, where every-one drove around in Mercedes."

"It's true England is better off than Sierra Leone," David responded. "But there are still poor people here. There are poor people everywhere in the world. In fact, more people are poor than rich."

My heart sank. If I didn't get an education soon and I remained in England, I would become a street person, having to beg like in Sierra Leone, but with one big difference: I'd be out in the cold and the rain.

Right after dinner that night, I asked Yabom to take the

colored magnetic letters off the fridge. So far, I hadn't tried very hard to learn the alphabet, because I hated pushing the letters around with my fake metal fingers. As David and Mariama cleared the table, I whispered for Yabom to bring the letters to my room. I asked her to help me take the contraption off. Then we sat cross-legged on the floor as I arranged the letters with my arms on the floor. It took me about an hour and a half, with several mistakes that Yabom had to correct, but I finally got the letters A to Z in the right order.

Yabom was very pleased. "Tomorrow we'll start to spell some English words," she said.

Our spelling sessions went well, but a week or two later Yabom asked me a question that shocked me. "Mariatu, who is Bill?"

I didn't know how to reply. I looked over at Mariama, who glared back at me.

The three of us were in Mariama's living room. When Mariama returned from her job with the government that day, she had asked Yabom, who was helping me with the letters, to come with her into their bedroom. I switched the television on and watched music videos until they returned. Then Mariama switched off the TV while Yabom took a seat beside me on the couch.

"Mariatu, who is Bill?" Mariama repeated, not nearly as nicely as Yabom.

A part of me hoped they already knew about Bill. After all, Yabom had been phoning Freetown regularly to give the camp progress reports on my treatment and to ask them to pass on the information to my family. After one conversation, Yabom reported that Marie, Alie, and Adamsay had moved to a small village outside Masaika, about a one-hour minibus drive from Freetown. They'd got the money to move from someone in Canada, Yabom said. "So how can she and Mariama not know about Bill?" I asked myself now.

Mariama drummed the sides of her chair with her fingers.

"Mariatu, who is Bill?" Yabom asked again. "Please tell us."

I took a deep breath and then, for the next hour, explained to Yabom and Mariama how Bill had come into my life and my family's life.

"Why didn't you tell us about Bill earlier?" Mariama demanded when I finished.

"I thought you already knew about him," I replied. "Besides, it's not like he wants me to move to Canada."

Yabom sighed. "Mariatu, he *does* want you to move to Canada. He's agreed to bring you to Canada."

I tried hard to hide my excitement. Mariama, Yabom, and David had done so much for me; I didn't want to hurt their feelings. But my spirits soared on hearing Yabom's news. I can't explain exactly why, since all I knew about the strange place called Canada was that salt fell from the sky, but I knew somehow that Canada was where I belonged.

"When does Bill want me to move to Canada?" I asked.

"Mariatu," Mariama scolded, "your prosthetic hands will be available any day now. You need to learn how to use them. You still need treatment here. You can't leave England."

I could feel my face grow hot. "But I want to go to Canada," I said. "I'm only in England for six months. What happens after that? Can I go to Canada then?"

"There is a strong chance you will be able to remain in England," Yabom said, slipping her arm around my shoulder. "Mariama's family is willing to sponsor you, and once you get used to your prosthetic hands, you can go to an all-girls school."

"Why?" I yelled. My response startled me as much as it did Yabom and Mariama. But I couldn't hold my anger inside any longer. "Why do I have to wear these things?" I demanded, holding up my metal hands. "I hate them! I can do everything I need to do without them, and better. I want to go somewhere else. I want to go to Canada!"

"Don't be so ungrateful," Mariama scolded. "You have an opportunity here that children at that camp of yours back in Freetown can only dream of."

I stood up and stomped. "I didn't ask for anything that happened to me, but I *am* asking to go to this place called Canada."

I ran straight to my bedroom, where I tore off the device and threw it on the floor. Yabom, who had followed right behind, tried to console me.

"Leave me alone," I yelled, pushing her toward the door. Yabom looked scared as my arms flailed wildly. I lashed out at her in a fury, just as I had done with Abibatu the night she prevented me from taking painkillers to kill myself and my baby. Yabom took several steps backwards to avoid my attack. When she did, I slammed the door in her face.

I stepped back, breathing erratically, until I bumped into the bed. I slid down to the floor, buried my head in my arms, and cried.

Eventually my tears stopped, but I remained in my room until the apartment fell silent and the others had gone to bed.

No one checked in on me or wished me good night. I guess they hoped I too had gone to sleep, and that by the next day my anger would have subsided.

My anger did go away, but not my determination to move to Canada. Despite Mariama and David's pleas that I remain in England, my mind was made up. Yabom, recognizing that further argument was pointless, began the process to acquire my Canadian visa.

One morning we took the Underground to the offices of the Canadian High Commission.

"I'm sorry," said a nice young woman, "but you need to return to your place of birth and apply from there to come to Canada."

"But she can't return to Sierra Leone," implored Yabom. "There's a war going on. She may never leave again."

This wasn't entirely true. It was now February 2002, and President Ahmad Tejan Kabbah had declared the war over just a month earlier.

"The rules are she must apply from Sierra Leone," the woman said politely. "There is nothing I can do from here."

"Then I will go home!" I announced to Yabom as we walked back to the Underground station.

"You may never leave again if you do," Yabom warned me. "Mariama and David are right. England is your opportunity. Going back to Sierra Leone is a great risk. There isn't even a Canadian consulate in Freetown—I don't know where this woman expects you to fill out the paperwork. You'll likely never leave Freetown again. Is that what you want?"

I waited until we were nestled beside each other on the

Underground, what Britons call the Tube. "I know in my heart of hearts I do not belong in England," I whispered to Yabom as I slipped my arm through hers. "I can't explain how I know this, but I do. I've known other things in my life, including that the rebels would come when they did. I tried to speak up in the past, but I always gave in to what older people wanted. This time, I want you to trust me. I can do almost anything now without my hands. I don't need these fake hands. And I want to see my family. Somehow, I will get that visa for Canada, and it will be in that country, which snows, that I will go to school and make something of myself."

"All right, Mariatu," Yabom said. "I will trust you. After all, this is your life. I will help you whatever way I can."

CHAPTER 16

Since my outburst, Yabom, Mariama, and David had given up trying to force me to eat by holding a fork between my fake fingers or to go for walks wearing the contraption. Slowly, they stopped protesting when I'd say: "Not today. Let's practice tomorrow."

In turn, I showed them that I could tie the laces on my running shoes, do up the zippers on my sweaters and jackets, and twist off jar lids and bottle tops using just my arms and teeth. I even started to cook my own food, mostly rice with hot peppers, chicken, and fish that Yabom and I bought at the market.

"I guess we made a mistake thinking the prosthetic hands would benefit you," David said sympathetically one night.

"No," I replied. "Maybe one day I'll get used to wearing them. But for now, I like doing things on my own. Thank you for your help, David. I learned a lot in England."

And I really had, even though the adults viewed my experience as a failure. I could read some English now, including street signs I recognized. I knew my numbers up to 100. But most of all, I had found the self-confidence in England to listen to my inner voice and speak up for what I needed and wanted.

I left London for Freetown on another rainy day. In my carry-on suitcase were my new plastic prosthetic hands, carefully wrapped in tissue paper. The ones I had been fitted for had replaced the metal device. But while my plastic hands were smaller and lighter, and fit snugly around my arms, I still could do more things without them.

Another thing I had discovered about myself in London was that I loved fashion. Packed alongside my prosthetic hands was a pair of black leather boots with stiletto heels. "Where will you ever wear those things?" Yabom had said when I asked her to buy them for me. "And how will you walk in them?"

In fact, I'd worn them everywhere. By the time I left London, I'd come to enjoy walking around the city, with my arms stuck in the pockets of a navy blue wool coat that actually fit, and wearing one of Mariama's silk scarves and those fancy boots.

Once we were seated on the airplane, I slid the blind down over the window beside me. I didn't want to see outside as we accelerated and took off, getting closer and closer to the clouds and then going through them. Every bump of turbulence saw me leaping for Yabom's arm and squeezing it tight.

Most of the other passengers slept on the airplane, but I dared not even close my eyes for fear the plane might crash. I listened attentively to every word the flight attendants spoke in English; I even understood some of what they were saying. I ate a tiny bit of my plain chicken and potato dinner. And then, just before we were set to land, I put on some makeup. I was nearly 15 now, and in London Yabom had let me try on her makeup. Before we left for Freetown, Mariama had bought me some lip gloss, pink eye shadow, and brown eyeliner for my very own, as well as a small case to carry the makeup in.

It was nearly midnight when Yabom and I arrived at Lungi International Airport, located across the Sierra Leone River from Freetown. Despite the late hour, the airport was bustling with porters and customs officers. One of the officers stamped my green Sierra Leone passport and then waved me through.

Outside the airport, young boys whistled at Yabom and me, thrusting their hands out for money. Both the hot, humid air and the sight of the boys hit me like a brick. These were kids like me, with family depending on them to earn a few leones to buy vegetables and rice. The airport was a good place for them to be; newly arriving foreigners, mostly employed by aid organizations, were often generous after their long flights.

Yabom gave a boy some leones to put our suitcases on a buggy and escort us to one of the waiting taxi-minibuses. About 15 of us, all foreigners except for Yabom and me, squeezed onto one bus.

The taxi drove right onto the ferry. When we were midway across the river, I got out of the bus and walked to the railing. I inhaled the familiar air, thick with the smells of burning coal and hot spices. "I'm home," I thought. I smiled, but then a cold shiver ran through me. "What if I don't ever leave Sierra Leone again? I just can't go back to a life of begging." A part of me felt at that moment I had made a terrible mistake by returning.

I didn't share these feelings with Yabom when I returned to the taxi. She had dozed off, and I awakened her only when we reached the other side and I saw her husband there to greet us. He loaded our luggage into a beat-up old car he had borrowed from a friend. I jumped in the back seat, while Yabom sat up front beside her husband.

The streets were alive even at this late hour, with people standing by fires frying cassava or trying to sleep on straw mats right on the cement or on the dirt road. I was very tired, and I was just about to fall asleep when Yabom's husband turned left after the Freetown clock tower.

"Where are you going?" I asked, suddenly alert and leaning forward.

"To our home," said Yabom.

"But I want to go back to the camp," I exclaimed.

"You can't, Mariatu," Yabom said, swinging around to face me. "On this, I must put my foot down."

"Why?" I asked. "I want to see my family!"

"But your family has moved to a village near Masaika," she answered.

"Only a few members of my family have moved," I cried out. "I still have relatives and friends at Aberdeen. Please take me there."

"Listen, Mariatu," Yabom said, softly yet sternly. "In this country, there is much suffering still. The war may have ended, but many, many people are homeless, still unable to return to their villages. Many, many people are injured like you. Sierra Leoneans may appear to be happy for your good fortune in going to England and now Canada, but deep down they are jealous. They want what you have. And they will do things, like hire women who practice witchcraft to cast spells on you so that bad fortune comes your way."

"I am not scared of these people," I said. "No one I know

would want evil to come to me. Not after everything I have been through. Take me back to the camp."

Yabom gazed at me silently for a few moments. "Mariatu," she said eventually, "I want to help, but you have to listen to me."

"And you have to trust me," I said, raising my voice. "You said in London you would. I want to go to Aberdeen!"

"Let her go where she wants," Yabom's husband cut in. "She's old enough to decide."

He turned the vehicle into a bumpy back alley lined with potholes, and before long we merged back onto the road that led to Aberdeen.

As we pulled up alongside the camp, I could see the burning fires. I heard people talking and dogs barking.

"I'll go in by myself," I said to Yabom, who had jumped out of the car and opened the door for me.

"Against my better judgment, I will trust you," she said. "I will come to see you in a few days. You're going to be all right, Mariatu. You are going to be all right."

I pulled up the handle of my suitcase and slung the long strap of my carry-on bag over my shoulder.

"Have a nice stay with your husband," I said to Yabom as I turned to enter the camp. "We'll be back together soon, and going to Canada. Don't you worry about that!"

"Hello! Hello!" I called out.

Mohamed, Ibrahim, Abdul, and Fatmata were really happy to see me when I woke them up. I knew from Yabom's calls home that the couple now had a daughter, Mariatu, named after me.

161

Fatmata folded me into her arms, sobbing. Mohamed joked around as usual. "You just couldn't live without me," he laughed. "Maybe you and I should get married."

"Ha, ha," I said, making a face. But I had to admit that he looked smashing in a white tank top and pants. "What happened to you while I was away?" I teased. "You've become a movie star!"

"A what?" he asked.

"Never mind," I said, embracing him. I had forgotten for a moment that Mohamed had never seen a television program or a movie.

For the first little while at the camp, I was able to feed everyone quite well, buying fish and goat with some money David and Mariama had given me. I bought a big bag of rice at the market that Abdul and Fatmata had to carry home together on their heads. We got some vegetables too, and avocado, pineapple, coconut, and plantain, although the pickings at the market were slim. Fatmata explained that many of the crops had been destroyed during the war, and farmers were only slowly returning to their work. Even if you could afford food in Freetown, that didn't mean you could escape starvation.

Not long after my return, I went to visit Victor. Several members of the theater troupe had moved away, he told me. Some had returned to their villages; others had received houses built by the Norwegian nonprofit group, just as Adamsay, Marie, and Alie had.

"The government is moving people to these houses," said Victor worriedly, "but they're far, far from their home villages. Some members of the troupe went alone to these places, without family or friends. It's just not right."

The theater troupe, he said, was also slowly losing money. Now that the war had ended, nonprofit groups weren't giving the troupe as much support. "I'm doing what I can," said Victor. He explained that he was writing a report about the benefits of theater in the emotional healing of both victims of the war and child soldiers.

Ten members of the troupe remained at the camp. On weekends, we would meet at the center, as in the past, to perform some skits, dance, and sing. But mostly, we'd sit around and talk.

"How was England?" my friend Memunatu asked me one day.

"Very cold," I replied. "You wouldn't have liked it."

Even though I hadn't believed Yabom when she said people would be jealous and out to get me, I didn't say too much about England or Canada to my friends and family. I'd realized soon after returning to the camp how incredibly lucky I was to be able to leave. I didn't want to make others feel worse about their situation.

"Come on, it must have been more than that!" Memunatu said. "Where are your new hands? I don't see you wearing any."

I didn't know how to reply. There was now a nonprofit group based at the camp fitting amputees with metal devices like the one I'd had in England, as well as plastic hands, feet, and legs. People were using their prosthetic hands to eat, drink, cook, and clean themselves. But I felt most comfortable doing things on my own, with the body parts I had remaining. I think I had felt so different from everybody else when I had

Abdul that now I desperately wanted to blend in. When I'd hidden my arms and walked around London in those tall black boots, I'd felt stylish, like I belonged in the city.

Comfort arrived at our tent one afternoon, plopped herself down on a stone, and announced that she, not Yabom, would be organizing my trip to Canada. "And I'll be coming with you," she grinned. I tried not to show my dismay. I had come to love Yabom like a mother.

Bill was sending me about $50 a month, which was enough, combined with my remaining money from London, that I didn't need to beg anymore.

It took a few months for Comfort to make the arrangements for my Canadian visa. Yabom was right: there was no Canadian consulate or Canadian government office in Freetown, so I had to travel to the neighboring country of Guinea to complete my application. Comfort accompanied me on the short flight. But unlike Yabom, she didn't let me hold on tight to her arm as we took off.

"Mariatu, you've flown so much now, you should be used to this," she laughed. She lifted my arm and put it back on my lap.

Shortly after our return, Comfort informed me that we were scheduled to leave for Canada in a few days.

"But I want to visit my mother and father," I protested. "I need more time. Why didn't you tell me earlier?"

"I only received the airline tickets today," she replied. "I didn't know either. So pack your things and get ready."

It was too far to travel to visit my mother or my grandmother, whom I wanted to hug one more time; my grandmother was old by now, and I feared she might die before

I returned to Sierra Leone. However, I decided I would visit Marie, Alie, and Adamsay in their new village. I didn't tell Comfort my plan, as I thought she'd say no to that too. I had a young man from the camp named Alusine take her a message as I flagged down the poda-poda headed to Masaika, the nearest big village.

It shouldn't have taken more than an hour to reach the village, but the road hadn't been maintained during the 11-year civil war. It was full of potholes so deep that the minibus often had to swerve into the thick elephant grass to avoid sinking. Even though I had left the camp in mid-morning, I didn't reach my destination until late afternoon.

Adamsay, Marie, and Alie's new village, located right off the main road, was a series of 10 new clay huts with tin roofs. The place didn't have a name yet, and my relatives knew few of their neighbors.

"I recognized a couple of people from the camp," Marie told me. "But we know no one well. Our family is now all over the place," she lamented. "We live among strangers. It's not right that I have to ask the woman grinding cassava beside me her name."

Marie, Alie, and the others had tilled and planted a new farm. The crops wouldn't be ready for another year, so they were using the money Bill sent me while I was in England to buy produce. There was a lake not far off where Alie did a lot of fishing.

I had planned to stay with Adamsay and my aunt and uncle all night long. But just as some boys had lit a big bonfire and the girls were donning grass skirts for dancing, Alusine, the boy from the camp, showed up.

"You have to come now," he said, breathing heavily from running.

I stood up quickly, in shock. Even in the firelight I could see he was covered from head to toe in red clay dust. "How did you get here?" I asked.

"I took a poda-poda, but it stopped in Masaika for refueling," he replied, still panting. "Gas is so scarce, the driver was told it could be an hour or two before some was available. I ran from there."

Adamsay was looking sadly off into the fire. We both knew Alusine's presence would cut my visit short.

"Comfort says you must return to Freetown now," Alusine continued. "She gave me some money to bring you home. You have to fill out some paperwork in the morning or you'll miss your flight."

"It isn't for another two days," I said.

"Comfort says to come. You have to come now."

I sat down in front of Adamsay and put my forehead against hers. "I love you," I whispered. "I always will. And soon it will be your turn."

CHAPTER 17

I actually watched as the airplane descended into Toronto's Pearson International Airport. "I can't see anything except white," I exclaimed as I peered out. "Are we dead?"

"No," Comfort laughed. "We're just going through the clouds."

We'd been traveling for about 19 hours. The best outfit I owned, an Africana red, yellow, and green docket-and-lappa, was now well wrinkled. I felt dirty, even though I had washed my face and brushed my teeth three times since boarding the flight from London to Toronto.

The plane dipped. "Whoa," I yelped, grabbing Comfort's arm and burying my head in her neck.

She didn't push me away this time. "It's just turbulence," she said. "Look now." She pointed out the window.

I gasped at the sprawling city below. It was so big! My eyes caught a large patch of green, followed by brown cement houses and then more green. "I'm going to like Canada better than England," I thought. "Already I can see color."

Inside the terminal, a customs official fingered through my passport, pausing to look at the visa. "Welcome to Canada," she said with a smile.

As we walked out into the Arrivals area, I braced myself for the first sights and smells of this new land. What I got instead were voices: voices calling my name, then blinding camera flashes and people thrusting their arms out to touch me.

"What's going on?" I asked Comfort.

"They are journalists," she replied.

"But what do they want with me?" I asked.

"I guess they are fascinated by your story."

I shrank behind Comfort as she smiled for the cameras. But it wasn't her picture the journalists wanted, it was mine. The cameras stopped flashing.

"Come on, Mariatu," she turned to whisper in my ear. "We'll find Bill and be rid of all this."

Two men in uniforms walked up to me and said hello in English. I was scared at first. Police in Freetown are usually rough, and these two men, with their serious expressions and their stiff, strong walks, looked like police officers too. When they told Comfort and me to follow them, I thought I was in trouble. Maybe they knew I didn't belong in Canada. After all, I was a poor Sierra Leone village girl who used to beg for food.

But these police seemed nice. They walked on either side of us, protecting Comfort and me from the journalists. They directed us to the very back of the waiting area, to a tall blond man. Beside him were a blonde woman and a boy about the same age as me. "Hello," the man said, shaking Comfort's hand. "I'm Bill."

Bill's wife, Shelley, and son, Richard, each gave me a hug. Bill slipped a gold chain with a charm on it around my neck. As he and Shelley talked to the journalists, I ran my right arm over the smooth gold. No one had ever given me jewelry before. A few minutes later, we all posed for a photograph. I smiled, following Comfort's lead.

It was the heat that struck me first when we got outside. Toronto was warm, like Sierra Leone. Toronto was humid too, just like home. The air smelled fresh, as if there had been a shower.

"Where is the snow?" I asked Comfort when we were tucked beside each other in the back seat of Bill's minivan. I'd never known anyone who owned their own poda-poda, but here many people seemed to be driving them.

Comfort laughed. The snow came in the winter, she said, which was still a few months away. "Don't worry, Mariatu. It will get very cold."

I wasn't sure how much Comfort really knew about Canada. The only place she'd ever been outside of Sierra Leone was Guinea, when she'd accompanied me to get my visa. But I didn't argue. I had to trust her wisdom as I didn't speak English very well and couldn't ask Bill directly.

Comfort rolled down my window, and as we drove I gazed out at the green fields of grasses and funny dark green trees with leaves that looked like needles. "Where's all the garbage?" I asked Comfort at one point. Freetown's garbage trucks had stopped running during the war, and the streets were filled with litter, everything from empty cigarette packages to broken plastic bottles.

"They throw everything away in plastic bags here," Comfort replied in Krio. "People buy whatever they want in

169

North America, and when they don't want it anymore, the garbage trucks take it away."

Her words made me scared. "What if I am not what this Canadian family expects?" I asked myself. "Will they get rid of *me*?"

On the street where Bill and his family lived, it was so quiet at night that I could hear crickets, just like back in Magborou. As in England, I had my own bedroom, with a single bed and a fluffy patchwork quilt that Comfort said was a bedspread for when the nights got chilly. A big window framed with frilly white curtains faced out into a forest.

The sun seemed to shine all the time in Canada, and we went for long walks in the hills. Shelley made us Western-style lunches and dinners of grilled cheese sandwiches, pizza, spaghetti, and salads.

After a few days of getting settled, Bill told me we'd been invited to a party. On the way there, he and Shelley took me to get my hair braided. The woman who did my hair was black-skinned, though she didn't speak Temne. I understood little of what was being said, but I liked getting the colorful ceramic beads woven into my hair.

When we were finished, we drove to another part of the city. Bill pulled up in front of a two-story house and a Sierra Leonean woman with a wide smile opened the front door.

"Welcome!" she said in Temne, her eyes sparkling.

Behind her stood a tall older man with short hair. "Come in, come in," he beamed, opening his arms.

A grin crossed my face as I stepped inside. I was back home, or so it seemed. Kadi and Abou Nabe's house was full of

Sierra Leonean wood carvings and paintings, and photographs of people wearing traditional Africana outfits and headpieces. As they led me through their kitchen, I smelled the rich, spicy aromas of simmering Sierra Leonean dishes. In the backyard, I could hear children laughing.

I had one of the best times of my life that afternoon. I kicked a soccer ball around with some of Kadi and Abou's nieces and nephews. I met and talked about Sierra Leone and Magborou with some girls my own age, who had grown up not that far from where I did, in a town called Makeni.

One of the girls told me that Kadi and Abou had been living in Canada since before the war. When the fighting started, they had brought many of their family members to Toronto to escape the violence. The girl explained to me that a summer backyard party in North America is usually called a barbecue, and that people cook hot dogs, hamburgers, and steaks on coal- and gas-burning outdoor stoves. She laughed. "In Sierra Leone we cook all our food that way. Every day is a barbecue!" she kidded.

"Don't worry," Kadi jumped in, sitting down across from me. "We have chicken and hot dogs for those who want to eat Western-style, and Sierra Leonean food for you! I bet you miss home."

By the time we left, it was close to midnight. Kadi and Abou hugged me goodbye and invited me to come back soon.

When I fell asleep that night, my head was filled with happy thoughts. I really loved being around Kadi, Abou, and their family and eating Sierra Leonean food again. My mind soon flooded with so many thoughts of home.

It felt as if I had just drifted off to sleep when I felt someone shaking my shoulder. It was Bill. He had turned the light on in my room and was sitting on the corner of the bed, his index finger to his lips to say: "Shush."

Bill pointed silently at my clothes, then at a small backpack. He smiled and said, "I'm taking you to see Kadi and Abou again."

Although my English was poor, I understood. It was still dark outside, but I didn't care what time it was. Bill left the room as I changed. He then thrust a carton of juice and a banana into my arms before we got into the car and left.

When we arrived at Kadi and Abou's house about an hour later, Kadi was waiting in the driveway. She explained in Temne that Bill wanted me to spend the day with her. "You are more than welcome," she said. "Some of the girls from yesterday will be home for the day, too."

Bill handed Kadi my backpack, which I had tossed in the back seat of the car. He gave me a hug goodbye and hopped back into his automobile. I had an eerie feeling as he drove away that I might never see him again.

CHAPTER 18

Kadi paced the kitchen. "Check to see if there is a message on the telephone," she said to Abou.

Abou lifted the receiver. "Nothing," came his gruff reply.

I was seated on a chair, my back up against the wall, heart pounding. It was well past dinnertime, and Bill was supposed to have picked me up by now. He'd called once during the day to say he would be a little late, but that was the last we'd heard of him.

I watched Kadi's daughter Ameenatu stroke her bulging stomach. She was due to give birth any day. She was sitting on the couch in the television room beside the kitchen, her feet up on a stool, fanning herself with a magazine. "Maybe he's run into traffic," she called out.

"But rush hour is finished," Kadi said, scratching her forehead. "Where could he be? Check if there is a message on the telephone," she asked Abou again.

This went on for another hour, until the telephone rang.

"Hello? Hello?" Kadi said, first in Krio and then in English. Her expression became grave as she listened, saying only a few words. "Yes. Okay. Yes." She hung up the receiver slowly.

"Mariatu, Bill wants you to stay with us a little longer," she said, getting down on her knees and rubbing my legs.

"Because he doesn't like me," I said with a sigh, thinking back to my initial worries that Bill might not like me.

"No, Mariatu," Kadi reassured me. Then she gave me the whole story: Bill had called her very early that morning, saying Comfort seemed determined to take me back to Sierra Leone for some reason, and that was why Bill had woken me when it was still dark outside and brought me to Kadi's house. "Bill wants you to stay in Canada and go to school," Kadi said. "He hoped he could convince Comfort if he had a few hours to talk with her alone."

"But that didn't happen?" I asked.

"Not yet," Kadi replied. "We have room, so you can sleep in the basement tonight with the other girls."

A smile crept onto my face at this suggestion. Suad, Haja, and Fanta were the girls I had met at the barbecue. We'd watched music videos during the day and we all prepared a Sierra Leonean rice dish together for dinner.

"Besides," Kadi continued, "right now you need some family and some Sierra Leonean cooking to help you get used to this strange country."

One week stretched into two, then three, then four. Bill called a few times to check up on me, but he never suggested I return. During one of their conversations, he told Kadi that Comfort had gone back to Sierra Leone. I don't know if she tried to find me first. I just don't know! This part of my story is confusing even for me.

Suad, Haja, and Fanta were only a few years older than me.

Each of them was related to Abou and Kadi, but I couldn't keep track of exactly how. I just called them all "the nieces."

The war in Sierra Leone had forced the nieces to move to Freetown. All of them had met up with the rebels in some way or another, but none of them had been attacked. Another big difference between us was that they had all been in school in Sierra Leone, and would be going to school here when summer turned to autumn. Everyone encouraged me to join them.

"School is fun," Suad said breezily. "I liked learning to read and hanging out with my friends."

I asked the three girls about school in Sierra Leone.

"All the kids around the same age met every morning in the schoolhouse," Fanta explained.

"I wore a green uniform that my mom sewed," said Suad. "The teacher taught us everything from how to read and talk in English to which water was safe to drink."

Unlike in Canada, where school is free, families in Sierra Leone have to pay for their children's school tuition fees and uniforms. Almost all of the lessons were taught in English, Haja told me, even though Krio, Mende, and Temne are Sierra Leone's languages. Haja said that was because English is the universal language. "Sierra Leoneans need to know how to communicate in business," she said. "Don't you want to have a job one day?"

Of course I did. I just didn't know what I would be good at, if anything.

One night I confided in Abou, who worked for the Canadian government, that my family was depending on me to support them. "I need to get an education, and then a job right away," I told him.

"Ahh, slow down, Mariatu." He winked. "I support most of my family back home, too. That's what everyone in Sierra Leone expects when one of their own moves to the West. But school will take years; it's better if you do it right, graduating from high school and then university or college. If you go out and get a job too soon, it won't be a high-paying position. Only your education will get you that."

"How did you get your job?" I asked.

"I went to university in Canada to study political science and economics."

"Do you think I'll ever be able to do that?" I asked.

"Mariatu, you can do whatever you put your mind to," he said, taking off his glasses and looking me straight in the eyes. "In North America, a lot of kids take getting an education for granted. But when you're from a poor country, you know what an education can do. It can open doors. You may not have hands, but you still have your mind. And I think you have a very sharp mind. Make the most of what you have and you will make your way in the world."

Despite Abou's words of encouragement, when Suad, Fanta, and Haja started getting up in the mornings to go to school, I rolled over and went back to sleep. As autumn stretched into winter, a great heaviness filled my heart. I spent many days staring out Kadi's living room window, watching as the leaves turned yellow and then red, and eventually fell to the ground. When the snow began to fall, it was nothing like I had imagined. The snowflakes were not heavy, like grains of salt, but light, like feathers that glittered in the sun. Occasionally my eyes would trace the path of an individual flake. I imagined

I was that snowflake in the big sky of so many others, and I tried to guess where I would land.

I was scared to go to school. Since Haja, Suad, and Fanta already had some education, they'd been placed in a higher grade. I would be alone, in a class with strangers. I dreamt of being able to read books and write, but I wondered how I would do it with no hands. With no one by my side to help me, I was afraid I'd make a fool of myself.

At night, I'd listen to the nieces recount their days and bemoan the homework they had to do. I'd shake my head when they asked if I wanted to go to school too. "Not yet," I'd reply. "Soon, I promise."

I enjoyed living with Kadi and Abou, whose home was always full of Temne-speaking Sierra Leoneans. Some, like the nieces, stayed for a long time. Others stayed just for a few days or weeks, until they found their own apartments. Our evening meals were always big plates of Sierra Leonean food. We'd eat together, before Kadi and Abou ran off to look at an apartment or to fill out some immigration papers for a new Sierra Leonean arrival. After the nieces had done their homework, we'd flop ourselves down on Abou and Kadi's comfortable couches and watch music videos. Some of them featured female hip-hop artists. Now, hip-hop I liked. All the women in the videos were black. Their music had a rhythm I could move to.

My mind often floated back to Sierra Leone. I missed Mohamed's jokes. I wished it was Marie cooking in the kitchen and not Kadi. I longed to feel Adamsay's warm body snuggled up beside me at night. I knew I had to get going, if not for me then for Adamsay, who was still in Sierra Leone. But she

177

seemed so far away. I wondered if she wouldn't be happier if I just came back to be with her.

One Saturday morning, I was jolted awake by five girls jumping on me. "Get up! Get up, lazybones!" Haja, Suad, and Fanta had been joined by two other female relatives, Umu and Kadiatu, or KK, who had just arrived from Sierra Leone.

Usually, the girls were quiet in the mornings, showering in the downstairs bathroom before heading upstairs for breakfast and then the bus to school. But this was the weekend. They had me surrounded on all sides and were poking me, playing with my hair, tickling my neck and stomach.

"Get up, sleepyhead!" Umu said, blowing into my ear.

"Not yet," I growled. I pulled a pillow over my head, but Suad grabbed it and started hitting Haja with it.

"Time to get up," Fanta sang, hip-hop-style.

Next they broke into a Temne song, one I remembered well from my childhood. "I was born a virgin and I am still a virgin," Umu sang.

"If that's what you say you are, prove it," the others chorused.

It wasn't a song you would hear in the West, but it was one of our village staples. The five girls sang another Sierra Leonean classic next.

"My boat is somewhere in Makeni," they chanted in unison, clapping their hands and slapping their knees to make the beat. "Oh, how I wish I could be with my boat."

I couldn't help but smile as I watched these young women, so bright-eyed and perky so early in the morning.

"It's not early," Umu laughed when they were done

178

singing. "You sleep all the time, so you don't even know what time of day it is anymore."

All the girls together pulled and pushed me into a standing position. "Brush your teeth and get ready," Fanta ordered. "We're going to braid your hair, and then we're going to the library."

Several hours later, I sat wedged between Suad and Haja in the back seat of Kadi's blue minivan. I wasn't sure what a library was, so I asked them. "When you finally go to school, you'll have to use the library," Umu said, wagging a finger at me. "The library is where you borrow books to help you study and learn."

"But don't be late returning the books," Kadi called over her shoulder from the driver's seat. "Haja, the last time you took a book out, you were a month late. I had to pay a big fine. I can't wait until all of you start working," she said, making a clicking sound with her tongue. "I'm planning on retiring on what you girls owe me."

"Of course, Auntie Kadi," said Fanta, who was sitting in the front seat. "Weeee love you," she sang.

Haja started playing with my hair, neatly braided with chestnut-colored hairpieces. "You know, Mariatu, you are actually very pretty."

"When we can see you," Suad teased. "Most of the time, you're buried underneath the blankets. You don't like us?"

"Of course I do." I smiled. No one had ever said I was pretty before. I never thought of myself that way.

"Good," said Fanta, turning around and grinning at me. "Because on Monday we all want you to go to school!"

Kadi continued in a serious tone. "I've enrolled you in an

English as a Second Language course. When you graduate, you'll go on to high school with the others next September."

"But Auntie Kadi—" I started to say.

"No," she interrupted. I could see her dark brown eyes in the rearview mirror. Her face was solemn, her expression no-nonsense. "It's time to get moving, girl!"

I knew by now that Kadi was like the mother of all the Sierra Leoneans in Toronto. Many people credited Kadi and her family with saving their lives.

"If Kadi says you have to do something," muttered Haja, "you better do it, or else she will send you back to Sierra Leone. She'll drop you off at the bus stop and say: 'Go. Find your way to the airport on your own.' Not something to look forward to."

I shivered at the thought. It was February, cold and gray and snowing outside.

As we made our way from the parking lot into the library, I ducked my face inside the collar of my bulky purple ski jacket, one of the items of clothing the imam at the local mosque had collected for Sierra Leonean refugees. When we got inside the front doors, Kadi took my arm and led me into the section of the library that she said was for children. It was a sunny room with fictional characters painted on the walls, including Mickey Mouse, Sleeping Beauty, Cinderella, and a turtle Kadi told me was named Franklin.

Kadi started pulling books off the shelves and piling them into my arms. "The best way to learn a new language is to start at the beginning," she said. "Read what the children are reading."

I must have been holding about 15 books by the time she

said, "That's enough for now." At a small table, we sat down on some children's-sized chairs.

"Okay," she said, picking up the top book. "This is a good one. It's called *Baby Sister Says No!*" She flipped it open. "Can you read any of these words?"

I shook my head.

"Mariatu," Kadi said sharply, "you can do better than that!"

I focused on the page. "This is an S, and here's a T," I said, pointing my arm at the letters.

"Very good," Kadi said. She turned the pages of the book, explaining that the story was about a funny porcupine-like creature whose baby sister won't let him do anything he wants. "Kind of like you girls living in my house," she joked.

"Now," she continued, picking up another book, "this book is about a monkey named George. And here's *The Sneetches*, by Dr. Seuss! I used to read this to my children when they were little."

Kadi was lost in thought for a moment. "The Sneetches don't want to associate with their own kind, because their own kind look different. Kind of like how the world works. Sometimes all we see are our differences. I can only dream of a time when that's not so." She sighed as she piled the books into a stack, then smiled. "When you can read these books to my granddaughter, you'll have made it. Let's go check these out." Ameenatu had given birth shortly after I arrived to a baby girl named Kadijah. If I didn't hurry up, the baby would catch up to my reading level. "Umu's right," I thought. "I need to get going!"

CHAPTER 19

On Monday morning, Kadi drove me to my first ESL class. "Most of the people there will be adults, and they come from countries where English is not spoken," she told me as we waited for a set of traffic lights to change. "All these people will be new to Canada too, and some have suffered greatly. Many countries have had wars, and many people escape those countries by coming to Canada. You'll see."

She was right. My classmates were young Asian women, grandmothers from the Middle East, and men from southern Africa. No one spoke English. The class was for beginners.

Kadi stayed with me for the first two days, sitting beside me at the back of the room. As we drove to the school and back, she followed the same route as the public buses, pointing out the bus stops along the way.

Over dinner at the end of the second day, she announced: "I have to go to work tomorrow!" Kadi also worked for the government, at a different location from Abou. She thrust some bus tickets into my pockets. "Just follow the directions I've been showing you and you'll be fine."

I gulped. "But Kadi, what if I get lost?"

"Then you get lost," she answered matter-of-factly.

Toronto is a big city. The population of 5 million is nearly the entire population of Sierra Leone. I imagined myself hopping on the wrong bus and ending up at the other end of the city, not knowing the telephone numbers of people to call, stranded, shivering in the cold.

On a blank piece of paper, Kadi wrote down the name of the bus I had to take to school and the street at which I needed to get off. On another piece of paper, she did the same for the return trip home.

"Show the piece of paper to the bus driver when you get on," she instructed. "He'll make sure you're on the right bus and let you know when to get off."

I was so nervous that first day I had to find my way all on my own. I dressed in a pair of Haja's snug jeans and a pink sweatshirt, then pulled on my purple ski jacket. I donned an oversized wool hat and wrapped a big wool scarf around my neck and face. All that showed were my eyes! I had taken the double-decker buses in London many times, but I'd always been with Yabom. Now I was alone.

I stood motionless at the bus stop, watching three buses slow down and then speed by, before I gained the courage to step forward, indicating to the bus driver that I wanted to get on. My arm shook as I gave him Kadi's instructions. The driver grunted "yes" and pointed to the seat directly behind him.

I was so afraid we were going in the wrong direction, I couldn't look out the window. After a while, though, the bus driver motioned for me to get off. As I stood up, I breathed a sigh of relief. There in front of me was the school.

The teacher just smiled as I sheepishly entered the class a half-hour late. She pointed for me to take a seat in front of her.

From that moment on, I listened to my teacher more closely than I have listened to anyone in my life. My mind would churn over the English words long after class ended. During breaks, I would spin around in my chair and practice talking to the person behind me. At first we communicated mostly through gestures, but soon we were saying English words to each other, and within a few months we were forming sentences.

At night, I'd read the children's books I'd checked out of the library. Soon I'd advanced from individual letters to identifying entire words like *the, and, girl, boy, doll,* and *sneetches.* I learned how to write these words in class. One of my proudest moments came when I wrote my name, MARIATU KAMARA, in a workbook with a pencil held between my arms.

I had come to Canada on a six-month visitor's visa. One Saturday afternoon I approached Kadi and Abou and told them I wanted to remain in school. "Maybe I'll go home when I can speak English," I said. They were so happy. That night we had a party with Kadi and Abou's entire family.

I applied for refugee status, eventually becoming a landed immigrant on humanitarian grounds; that meant I was a victim of war and had a better chance of a good life in Canada than back in Sierra Leone. My sponsors were Kadi, Abou, and a man named Alimamy Bangura from the Sierra Leone Immigrant, Resettlement and Integration Centre in Toronto, which Kadi and Abou had helped start.

On a muggy June evening 10 months after arriving in Canada, I graduated from my English as a Second Language course with a diploma. Our graduation ceremony took place in the school auditorium, and all of the students contributed potluck dishes for the feast afterwards. I made rice and fish with peppers. I couldn't wait to sample the Middle Eastern rice dishes and Cajun chicken from the West Indies.

Before we got to the food, though, each student had to give a short speech in English, on any topic he or she wanted. When it was my turn, my eyes scanned the audience until I found Kadi, Abou, and the nieces. "Thank you for giving me a home," I said, "and accepting me as one of yours. You are my sisters. I will always love you for the fun you bring to my life. I wouldn't be here, on this stage, getting my ESL diploma if it weren't for all of you." I thanked my ESL teacher and all the friends I had met in the class too. "Canada is a very nice place to live," I ended. "I'm glad it turned out to be everything I expected, and more."

CHAPTER 20

When September rolled around, it was time for high school. I wasn't alone this time. KK, Umu, and Mariama, Umu's sister who had just arrived from Sierra Leone, accompanied me on my first day, and it turned out that KK was in three of my four classes: English, science, and math.

I liked high school from the moment I stepped into the main foyer. The long, narrow hallways were lined with lockers and students of all nationalities, sporting cell phones, Walkmans, fashionable jeans, and purses. I seemed to fit right in. KK and I were the eldest in our grade nine class, though we are both so tiny that nobody guessed. Many of the students spoke English like me, with thick accents from foreign places.

Because of my disability, the school assigned me a special tutor. She sat beside me in every class, taking notes and working with me one-on-one to figure out math equations, define English words, and explain the procedures in biology class. I liked science and math best. I had a natural ability to count things out in my head, I learned— perhaps, I mused to Kadi one night, from my two years of begging in Freetown. If Abibatu needed four peppers for dinner, I knew I had to earn at least 500 leones while begging to pay for them. I don't like the sight of blood, but I wasn't squeamish in biology class when I had to dissect a frog or look at graphic pictures of the human body, probably because I had seen so much in the hospitals in Sierra Leone.

My tutor was very patient as she taught me cursive writing, with a pencil or pen held between my arms. Just like when I learned to print, my first major accomplishment was writing my own name: *Mariatu Kamara.*

My teachers gave me extra time to complete tests and examinations. I think I may have failed the first semester. While the other students received report cards with marks and written comments, my teachers merely said I was doing well.

But by June, I did get a report card, and I'd earned Cs across the board.

"This is a computer," said the resource center instructor, an older woman with glasses and short black hair. We were sitting at her cluttered desk, full of papers and computer parts. She had cleared away some of the debris to make room for a black laptop — my laptop — that the War Amps of Canada had bought for me.

It was winter 2004. I was still living with Kadi and Abou, but all five of us young women had moved upstairs into Ameenatu's bedroom, so that she and her family could take over the basement. While the nieces and I fought over the bathroom in the morning, we also shared clothes, boots, jackets, and purses.

I knew what a computer was, since the nieces used an older PC to do their homework in the living room. Several students brought laptops to school, too. The teachers forbade them to use their computers during class, but on break they'd sit by their lockers or go to the school library and type away. I couldn't help but watch as their fingers flew over the little keys. I wished I had fingers that could do that.

"This laptop," the instructor went on, "is designed for people with disabilities." The mouse was shaped like a big ball, so that I could easily maneuver it with my arms.

I watched the icons for Word and Internet pop onto the screen. I moved the ball, and the instructor showed me how to hit the little arrow on the blue W. A blank page appeared on the screen.

It was hard at first to hit the keys. Even though the keyboard was big, it was not easy to master hitting one letter at a time. An hour later, when the instructor said our time was up, all I had on my screen was a mismatch of letters and numbers.

That evening, when the nieces were downstairs watching a movie, I sat on my mattress and played with my new computer. It took some experimenting, but I finally managed to spell out a complete sentence: *My name is Mariatu Kamara. I live in Toronto, Canada, and like it here very much.*

Once I became proficient on the laptop, the instructor taught me how to connect to the Internet. There was so much to explore, including websites that talked about the war in my country and chat groups where I could communicate with Sierra Leoneans living all over the world. I started sending emails, first to the nieces, but soon to friends I had met at school.

One day, Kadi gave me Bill and Shelley's email address. "I haven't heard from them in a long time," she said, "but you might as well try."

Hi Bill and Shelley, I wrote. *You may remember me, it's Mariatu Kamara. You helped bring me to Canada.*

I didn't hear back for about a month. When I did, their email made me very sad.

Richard, they told me, had been killed in a car accident.

Bill and Shelley also explained how they had come to know about me in the first place. They wrote that on a sunny Sunday afternoon, they were driving in the countryside. Shelley read aloud a newspaper article about the war in Sierra Leone. That article featured me. Afterwards, Richard had turned to Bill and asked him to do whatever he could to help me, including bringing me to Canada if he could.

Bill and Shelley also told me that Comfort hadn't wanted me to stay in Canada. They said that they had been fighting with her from the moment we arrived. Comfort, according to the email, wanted to remain in Canada too, and had threatened to take me back to Sierra Leone if she didn't get her way. That's how, Bill and Shelley now revealed, I had ended up with Kadi and Abou. Bill and Shelley wanted me to stay in Canada and have a shot at life, which they felt I wouldn't have in Freetown.

When I finished reading the email, I closed my laptop and thought about sweet Richard, who had walked in the hills with me, introducing me to chipmunks, squirrels, and even a deer with a fluffy white tail. He was responsible for bringing me to this country, and now he was dead. Bill and Shelley had written that Richard was in heaven, smiling down on me. Maybe he was with Abdul and Santigie. Maybe they were all smiling down on me. I hoped so.

And then I thought about Comfort. If what Bill and Shelley said was the truth, then she had lied to me.

"Hmmn ... Whatever the truth is," I thought as I went to sleep that night, "I'm here, in Canada, getting an education. Bill, Shelley, Richard, and Comfort all did a good thing."

CHAPTER 21

It was late spring 2005, and I was seated in the library of G.L. Roberts Collegiate and Vocational Institute. I was hiding my shaking knees under a big round table, afraid to look up into the eyes of the journalists who were waiting to talk with me.

In a few minutes, in the auditorium down the hall, the famous Canadian rock band Sum 41 would take the stage, along with some lesser-known bands, in a benefit concert to benefit, well, me. The students at my high school, working with the students at G.L. Roberts, had organized the event.

Kadi, as always, was beside me.

"I'm scared," I whispered to her as the first journalist approached.

"Don't be," Kadi whispered back. "You've talked to the media a thousand times before. You're an old pro!"

I'd met with journalists many times, that was true. But I was more nervous this time than ever before, and for good reason. These would be the first interviews in which I answered the questions myself, in English, without a translator telling most of my story. My mind had run through all the possible answers I could give to the questions I thought would be coming. And not one of those answers felt right to me.

Every so often a student at my school had mentioned reading a newspaper article about me. I'd never read any of the articles myself, so I would just nod and thank them for their interest.

Then one of these students suggested to our World Issues teacher that we discuss the articles in class. The teacher checked it out with me, and I said yes.

As the teacher read the first article out loud, I wanted to melt in my seat.

After she read a second one, I wanted to run right out of the room.

When she had finished reading the articles, the teacher asked if I wanted to share anything else about my life experience with my fellow students.

A knot formed in my throat. "No," I croaked.

The students clapped. The bell rang. Class was over.

I dashed out of the room, even though several of my friends were waiting to talk to me, and ran straight to the washroom, where I was sick to my stomach.

Some of my classmates had followed me. They thought I was upset because I was reliving the bad things that had happened to me. A girl pulled out her cell phone and was about to call one of the nieces when I managed to say, "I'm okay. I just want to be alone for a while."

I was traumatized that day because I had learned for the first time that much of the information written in those articles was wrong. The most glaring mistake the journalists had made was stating that the rebels had raped me.

After my confession to Yabom in London, I never spoke of Salieu's assault on me again. Like many people who experience violence, I wrongly believed I had brought it on myself. I would say to myself: "If only I'd left the house that day Salieu came! If only I'd agreed to be his wife, he wouldn't have touched me until we were married!" I never wanted to utter Salieu's name again, let alone have to think about him, so I had shut him out of my head.

That day in school, I realized that a big lie had formed because of my silence. And now I didn't know what to do. Part of me wanted to correct the mistake while I had the chance. Another part of me felt it would be easier to say nothing. I swallowed hard as a reporter from the *Toronto Star* sat down opposite me.

"Hello," the woman began. "Are you excited about the concert?"

"Yes," I replied.

"You must be pleased to know that your dream of prosthetic hands will soon be a reality?" she asked.

"Yes," I said, more hesitantly.

That was the other reason I didn't want to talk to journalists: the benefit concert was to raise money to help buy me prosthetic hands, and I was still uncertain that I wanted them. The only people who knew of my concerns were Kadi and Abou, and they had encouraged me to give prosthetic hands another try.

Abou had explained that some prosthetic devices are attuned to your nerves and can move accordingly, meaning if I twitched a muscle as if to pick up a pen, the way I would if I had fingers, the prosthetic hand would sense this and pick up the pen. The prosthetic hands I'd received in England didn't do that.

"Please don't tell me they're made out of metal," I had moaned.

"No," Abou had replied, laughing. "They look just like real hands." He showed me a photograph of them on the Internet, and sure enough they did. But the hands cost nearly $30,000.

Kadi had asked my tutor whether I might do better at school if I learned to write my examinations along with the other students, using prosthetic hands. I was still mostly pulling in Cs, and Kadi felt I could do better. The tutor, who thought it was worth a try, told the principal how much money was needed, and the principal told the student council. The students had pulled together this event.

I was scared that if people knew the truth about my rape or my dislike of prosthetic hands, they would abandon me. I didn't want to let them down, either. Everyone seemed so proud of me.

Just a few weeks earlier, I had completed reading Shakespeare's *Romeo and Juliet* for my grade 11 English class. I cried tears of joy when I put the book down. I was finally at the same level as my peers.

After I'd told my drama class about the theater troupe at the camp, my classmates wanted to know more about our performances. Our drama teacher didn't like us chatting, but behind the curtains I'd whisper to my friends about HIV/AIDS and the part I'd played of a mourning village woman.

"I wish *we* could do a play about our lives," one of the boys said.

"We could do plays about cutting and violent boyfriends and dieting," said one girl.

"Instead, we have to put on this boring stuff that only adults want to watch," another added. We all started to laugh.

"QUIET BACK THERE," the teacher yelled.

Everyone seemed happy that I was part of their lives. But I worried that could change in an instant.

None of the journalists in the library that afternoon asked questions about the war or about Abdul. I was relieved at the time, though afterwards I wished I'd been able to tell everyone the truth.

Before the concert began, I had to go onstage to say a few words. I was really nervous about that too.

"Hello, everyone," I said into the microphone. There was standing room only in the audience. "Thank you so much for doing this for me."

Beside me stood some of the band members from Sum 41. I hadn't done enough public speaking to risk making a joke. But I was thinking of one, something like "All you girls should come and meet these cute boys after." The girls in the front row already had their eyes glued to the band members' every move.

The concert was fun. I didn't feel like dancing, so I stood off to the side and watched. In between playing songs, some of the band members spoke about the impact of war on children and called for world leaders to do more to end the conflicts. I hadn't known until I came to Canada that there are wars all over the world, and that today children are the number one casualty. In many countries there are children like me, maimed by guns and knives.

As I was leaving the stage, a teacher I knew came up to me. "You should write a book," she said. "I'd make sure every one of my students read it!"

I mulled over the teacher's comment as we drove home that evening. She wasn't the first one to suggest a book about my life. I couldn't imagine many people would want to read such a book, even if I could figure out how to write it. At least, though, I fell asleep thinking, a book could dispel the myths that had built up around me.

On a warm April night in 2007, writing my book became a reality.

Kadi had announced a few days earlier that a journalist who'd interviewed me after I arrived in Canada wanted to do a follow-up story. Now the journalist, whose name was Susan, sat across from Kadi and me, asking questions about how I liked high school.

"Have you heard of Ishmael Beah?" Susan asked near the end of our conversation.

"No," I replied.

Ishmael was a former child soldier in Sierra Leone, Susan said, and he had published a best-selling book about his experiences.

"Best-selling book!" I exclaimed. "People in the West want to read about Sierra Leone?"

Susan nodded. Ishmael was going to be in Toronto the following week, she told me. My story would run beside his in a national newspaper, the *Globe and Mail.*

As she was leaving, Susan turned to me. "Mariatu, would

you like to meet Ishmael?"

I gulped. I thought of the boy soldiers who had cut off my hands. "I'm not sure," I replied. "Can I think about it?"

Many, many times I had thought back to those boy soldiers. Kadi and Abou kept me pretty sheltered from Sierra Leone politics, but I had learned through the Internet that a special court had been set up in Freetown to investigate some of the soldiers, including the leaders who had ordered rape, murder, and the amputation of people's hands.

What would I do if I was in that courtroom and had to testify? I asked myself. What would I do if I ever saw one of those boys who had hurt me?

At first I felt only anger. I wanted those four boys dead. I hoped the special court would order them killed.

But the anger made me feel sick, and over time I saw that taking a life was not the solution. They were kids, like me, who'd got caught up in something beyond their control. Maybe in the bush they'd thought of their parents and sisters, and felt alone and scared like I had.

There was nothing I could do, I realized, even if I wanted to. Even if those boys were right in front of me, I wouldn't be able to hurt them, not with my words or with my body. They might spend some time in prison, but there was no way I could allow myself to make them suffer. Instead, I imagined those boys standing before me as I said to them: "I hope you're very sorry for what you did to me. But I forgive you."

Susan called over the weekend to make sure I had seen her stories in the newspaper. At about eight o'clock that Sunday night, as I was sitting alone in my bedroom, I punched in

Susan's telephone number on my cell phone. If I didn't reach her, I vowed I'd take it as a sign not to go through with what I was about to ask.

Susan picked up.

"Hi, it's me, Mariatu," I said. "How was your weekend?"

"Good, and yours?"

"Fine. How are the girls?" She'd told me about her two young daughters.

"Good," she replied. I could sense she knew that I was procrastinating. "Everything okay, Mariatu?" she asked.

"I want to meet Ishmael!" I blurted out the words before I knew what I had done.

"I think I can arrange that," Susan said.

Three days later, I was standing in front of a big old church in downtown Toronto with Abou, Kadi, and Susan. Ishmael's publicist had said we could have a private session with him before his speech and book signing.

When I saw Ishmael, I breathed a sigh of relief. He didn't look at all like any of the boys from Manarma. He had a broad face, a high forehead, and curly hair. I instantly felt I had found a friend, odd as that seemed with a former child soldier.

Abou opened the conversation with Ishmael by talking about Sierra Leonean food. "I miss those cassava leaves and hot peppers," he joked as he bit into a coffee-shop sandwich.

Ishmael asked if I knew any Sierra Leoneans in New York City, where he lived. I did. Some of the kids from the refugee camp had moved there, and we discovered we had some friends in common. Next we talked about music. He likes rap, I prefer hip-hop.

"I want to write a book," I said to Ishmael as his publicist signaled that it was time for his speech to begin.

"What do you want to call it?" he asked.

"Hmm ... Maybe *Never Give Up on Your Dreams.* Is that a good title?"

"I think it's an excellent title." He smiled, then moved to give me a goodbye hug.

"Do you think anyone will want to read a book about me?" I asked.

"Yes," came his reply. "Yes."

CHAPTER 22

It's February 2008, and I'm back in Sierra Leone with Susan, Kadi, a woman from UNICEF Canada, and Sorious Samura, the filmmaker who made *Cry Freetown*, a documentary chronicling the brutal January 1999 invasion of Freetown by the rebels. I got the book deal: Susan and I were working on my memoir, and we have returned to Sierra Leone to finish and fact-check the book.

It's early in the morning on our second week in the country. Sierra Leone smelled just like I remembered: the air thick with aromas of open fires, spices, and the ocean, and bright, like a soft fluorescent light. I'm in Freetown. I crawled out of bed, opened the window, leaned out, and inhaled. Just as I was about to turn and wake up Kadi, my cell phone rang.

"Hello," I said after digging it out of my purse.

It was Sorious Samura on the other end. "You're going to meet the president tomorrow," he said.

The phone was crackling, and I wasn't sure I had heard him correctly. "I don't understand," I replied. "What did you say?"

"Mariatu, I've arranged for you to meet the president tomorrow. The president of Sierra Leone."

As Sorious went on to give me details of the meeting with President Ernest Bai Koroma, including how I should present myself to the leader of my native country, I thought back to the time, nearly nine years earlier, when I had first heard the word *president.*

"Mariatu, are you listening to me?" Sorious's voice broke into my thoughts.

"Yes," I said. "I have been listening. But I don't see how I can meet the president."

"All you have to do is tell him your story," Sorious said gently. "Can you do that?"

"I will think about it," I whispered after a long pause. "I will try to remember."

After my conversation with Sorious, I didn't feel like talking to anybody. I was too worried. What could I possibly say to the president? Why would he want to listen to me?

Susan and Kadi and I were going to Yonkro to visit my family. I had to get bathed and dressed or else we wouldn't make it to the village until midday. Kadi had awakened at the sound of the phone, and as she stumbled to the bathroom, she asked me who it was.

"Sorious," I replied. "He says we're meeting the president tomorrow."

"Good," Kadi said as she shut the door to the washroom. "He went to school with my brother. It will be nice to see him again," she called out nonchalantly. I then heard the sound of water running.

For a moment I laughed, thinking that everyone in Sierra Leone is either related to Kadi and Abou or knows them. But then my mind returned to the actual meeting with the president. Even the president being a friend of Kadi's brother did little to soothe my nerves. I said barely a word all the way to Yonkro.

I was still mulling over Sorious's call when we reached the tiny village outside Lunsar. As we got off the bus, the village children and a few women sang a song of welcome.

"Mariatu! Mariatu, is that you?" I swung around at the sound of my grandmother's voice. She was shuffling her way down the dirt road in an Africana wrap skirt and baby blue head scarf.

She had aged so much since I'd last seen her. Her face was wrinkled, her eyes sunken, and several of her teeth were missing. I realized she was using the long stick in her hands not only to prop herself up but to feel her way.

"I'm here, Grandmother," I called back, taking off and running into her arms.

We embraced, and then my grandmother clutched my face in her hands. "I never thought you'd come back," she cried. "But you did."

"I wanted to surprise everyone, Grandmother." Her brown eyes appeared blue, because of what I learned were cataracts. Cataracts could be fixed easily in Canada, but not for poor people in Sierra Leone. I realized my grandmother was now blind.

I hadn't told anybody I was coming home. A month earlier, I'd used part of the advance from my book deal to buy and ship to Sierra Leone a crate full of clothes, shoes, toothpaste, soap, and umbrellas. I'd talked to Marie and Alie on the telephone since then, but I'd given no hint that I was about to see them for the first time since I'd left six years before. I didn't want them to go out of their way, preparing big feasts or using the little money they had to take a minibus to greet me in Freetown. I wanted to spoil them instead.

We worked our way through the crowd of singers, and I led my grandmother to a small wooden bench by the side of my mother's hut. Four puppies snuggled up against our feet.

I laid my head on my grandmother's lap, the way I had when I was a little girl, as she stroked my hair and asked me about my life in Canada. I told her about Kadi and Abou and how much they had done for me. I broke into tears as I lifted my head and looked into her glossy eyes.

"Grandmother, I've been wanting to tell you something for a very long time. Remember how you told me that dreaming of palm oil means blood will spill by the end of the day?"

"Yes," she said.

"I had such a dream, the night before the rebels came."

"Tell me your dream," she said.

Over the next hour or so, I let everything out. I told my grandmother about my dream, about the rebels, about the boys' faces. I told her about the rape and about Abdul and how, even to that day, I blamed myself for his death. I told her about the amputee camp and begging, and about going to London and then Toronto.

When I stopped talking, my grandmother and I sat there in the shade, listening to some roosters crow. Some of the village kids were playing a game of hide-and-seek while two boys pushed a metal tire rim around with sticks.

"What would you have done if you'd been in Manarma

with me?" I asked my grandmother.

"If I had been there the morning of your very bad dream," she said after a pause, "I would have done what was customary. I'd have cast a spell to make those demons go away."

"What kind of spell, Grandmother?"

"We would have gone to the lake together and thrown a big rock into the middle of the still waters," she said. "We would have asked the spirits around us to leave those demons in our heads and not let them take the guise of the rebels."

"So you would have believed me?" I asked.

"Yes," she said. "But Mariatu, many things have changed because of the war. And witchcraft can't change the past. I wish a spell could have stopped the attack on you. But you have turned your hurt and pain into something positive. When those demons reappear, think about all the angels who have come into your life since then."

Sulaiman was one of those angels, as were Fatmata, Kadi, Adamsay, Abibatu, Mohamed … the list goes on. When it was Christmastime in Canada, Sulaiman had died. One morning he had woken up and had difficulty breathing. He wheezed and coughed and couldn't pull himself out of bed. He hadn't gone into the shop he kept in Freetown, selling needles, thread, and biscuits. Instead, he lay on his back all day. His wife, Mariatu, soaked his brow with a damp cloth.

Sulaiman's breathing became more labored, and a shooting pain ran up and down his arms. Mariatu tried to feed him using a big wooden spoon, but in the end his heart failed.

I was very sad to hear this news. Sulaiman was no more than 30 years old when he died, but he had spent all his money on medicine for my cousins and me after the rebel attack; he had no savings to pay for the doctor or the medication he needed.

When I learned of Sulaiman's death, I offered to pay for the 40-day funeral ceremony. In Sierra Leone we mourn the dead with festivities at the time of burial and again at the 40-day and one-year marks. Sulaiman's body was buried in Yonkro, where he and my father, Marie, and Abibatu had been raised. He was buried alongside my father, who had died from old age while I was living in Canada.

Leaving my grandmother, I slipped down the alleyway between two grass huts and came out into an open space, where women were cooking rice and boiling chicken in huge pots over several open fires. Mariatu was there, dressed from head to toe in black to indicate that she was in mourning.

A few women were rolling rice in sugar, making a dessert that is common in Sierra Leone. I handed one of the balls to Mariatu. "I'm sorry for your suffering," I said, looking down.

Mariatu answered as if she knew the guilt I was carrying. "Sulaiman never regretted helping you," she said kindly. "Never once."

Over the years, my mother had given birth to 10 children. She was still young-looking, but thin—too thin. Her Africana skirt was dirty, and her T-shirt was torn on one shoulder. I felt self-conscious in my silver hoop earrings and new white, blue, and pink Africana docket-and-lappa that Kadi had bought for me in Freetown to wear to Sulaiman's funeral.

My younger sister Mabinty and I had never met, but any onlooker would have known we were siblings. I looked into my own brown eyes when my mother introduced us, and saw my own smile spread across her eight-year-old face. We laughed as we threw our arms around each other. A minute later, though, Mabinty was crying.

"I'm sick, Mariatu," she sobbed. "I can't breathe, just like Sulaiman. Sometimes I have to stay in the hut all day, not moving."

I wondered if Mabinty had asthma, something I knew about from living in the West. In this remote village, halfway between Port Loko and Lunsar and well off the main road, I was sure she had never seen a doctor. Her life was probably just like mine had been before 1999, before the rebels.

Mabinty dried her tears as she showed me around the village. Before she was born, she said, rebels had burned down all the huts in Yonkro. The village men had rebuilt the place one clay brick at a time.

Back in the center of the village, we sat down in the shade of a hut to listen to the traveling imam, who was reciting verses from the Quran to mark Sulaiman's passing.

"It's better to have a goat and chicken than to give birth to a girl," the imam said to the 10 men sitting in a circle around him.

I rose to rejoin the women. "Many things have changed, Grandmother," I thought, "but some things remain the same."

As the day wore on in Yonkro, I grew increasingly quiet. My mind was churning over everything that I was seeing: my family's ripped and dirty clothes; the sadness in their eyes; the wilted stems of their crops, now that the rainy season creeps upon them for only a few weeks each year, rather than a few months, because of global warming. I hadn't noticed any of this when I lived in Sierra Leone. But now I lived in a place where many families drove two cars, bought new clothes every month, and dined out at restaurants regularly.

En route back to Freetown, I gazed out the window at the elephant grasses and swaying mango trees. I thought of Ibrahim, who was now living in Guinea, trying to find work, but with no luck. Adamsay was still in the little village outside Masaika, now mother to a five-year-old daughter named Kadija. Adamsay had never left Sierra Leone. No nonprofit group ever approached her again, and she sold any extra produce from her small farm on the side of the main road. She wanted to send her daughter to school but didn't have the money for the tuition or uniform. Not once, though, had she complained to me about her life. "I miss you so much," she had said when we saw each other. "I hope you have been doing what Marie asked of you: to always look forward!"

As the main road became congested with boys on motorcycles and women and children selling mangoes, coconuts, and plantains from big bowls they carried on their heads, I asked the minibus driver to stop at Waterloo, a small suburb of Freetown, where I wanted to visit Mohamed.

Mohamed, like everyone else, was flabbergasted to see me. He had a quizzical expression on his face at first. I didn't think I had changed that much, but my hair had been woven into a sleek shoulder-length style, and I was a little heavier than when I'd last seen him. I was wearing nice clothes, too, not tattered hand-me-downs from Father Maurizio.

"Yes, it's me," I said, laughing.

He grabbed my arm, pulling me into a long hug.

Mohamed looked so toned that, if he lived in North America, I'd have teased him that he had to be going to the gym every day. His wide smile, as always, showed off his perfect white teeth.

Mohamed's eyes sparkled as he plopped his four-month-old daughter Safia onto his lap. She was dressed in a crisp blue cotton dress with a matching bow in her hair.

"I fell in love," he said, beaming. "Can you believe it?"

I couldn't believe it. In my heart, Mohamed will always remain that joking older cousin who used to pull my hair and steal my food.

Mohamed lived in one of the small cement huts that a foreign nonprofit group had donated to some victims of the war. He showed me around the Waterloo suburb, which had been a displaced persons camp for amputees, like Aberdeen, during the war. Litter lined the ground like a carpet. Tin cans and the carcasses of dead dogs and cats filled the sewage ditches.

"I'm still begging at the clock tower," Mohamed told me. "But we don't make as much as before. There are so many of us on the streets that businesspeople usually just walk on past. The girls and boys coming home from school in their uniforms spit on us."

Uncharacteristically, Mohamed turned bitter as Sorious, who had joined us, began filming. "They used us," he hissed. "The government used the kids at Aberdeen to gain media and money from foreign countries. We've seen none of it. This is all we have." He swept his arms to indicate the huts. The one-room buildings were sheltered from the biting sun by mango trees, but Waterloo was nowhere near any farmland, and it was a half-day's walk to get to downtown Freetown and the clock tower.

Four years earlier, several members of the theater troupe had organized a march, shutting down the streets of Freetown for a whole day. They held up placards demanding that the president listen to their stories. "We need education, a shot at life!" the posters read. Many amputees took part, including Mohamed. In fact, he had been in the march's front line, linked arm in arm with other amputees, as the 1,000-strong crowd rounded the corner toward the presidential palace.

"Nothing happened," he told us angrily. "The government did nothing, just watched us screaming out to be heard." He stopped speaking for a moment. "You know, the kids around here play war games. They pretend to shoot and kill the rebels who cut off their parents' hands. Turn around, Mariatu," he said softly. "Return to Canada and don't look back."

In Freetown, Kadi, Susan, and I stayed at the Barmoi, a brand-new hotel filled with Western comforts, including a laundry service, television, air conditioning, and a restaurant serving pizza and spaghetti. The hotel was gated, with at least four uniformed Sierra Leoneans standing guard at any given time. Surrounding the building was a tall cement wall topped with barbed wire.

A week before our arrival, soccer superstar David Beckham had stayed at the hotel as part of his UNICEF visit. Now the place was full of middle-aged men with Australian, American, and British accents, there to work with the many charities in Freetown or to advise the government on how to enforce the payment of taxes.

Since being in Sierra Leone, I had learned that our country ranks at the bottom of the United Nations Human Development Index. The first week of my visit home involved my touring with UNICEF to see the organization's projects in the eastern region of the country. I met with many poor Sierra Leoneans. I held their babies. I laughed and I cried. I learned that fewer kids go to school in Sierra Leone than in any other country in the world. Sierra Leone has the lowest life expectancy of any country, with adults lucky to live until they're 40, compared to Canada, where people can live to 90 and still be healthy. Sierra Leone has few income-generating exports or commodities. The country has lots of resources, as I had learned from Yabom, including diamonds, bauxite, gold, iron ore, and manganese, as well as fresh water and fishing. Foreigners reap most of the profits, though.

"If I were a millionaire," I thought, "I'd hire a minibus and pick up Mohamed, Mabinty, Adamsay, Memunatu, Marie, Alie, Ibrahim, my grandmother, and all the others and put them on an airplane to Toronto. But I'm not. So how can I best help my family? How can I be of help to the people of Sierra Leone?"

Ishmael's book had inspired me to tell my story. When I heard him say during his Toronto speech, "What we need to hear next is the story of a girl from the war," I got excited. I felt I had found my purpose. I could contribute by telling the world about war, about family, about being a girl in Sierra Leone.

But now a part of me wanted to take Mohamed's advice and run far, far away, never again to return. My story was just one of thousands in Sierra Leone. What made it any different from anyone else's?

Another part of me wanted to stay in Sierra Leone with my family, living in Yonkro or the tiny village outside Masaika. If war had never come to my life, I might still be in Magborou, married to a boy named Musa. I was very confused after visiting my grandmother and Mohamed.

I walked outside and flopped down on one of the chairs around the hotel's sparkling swimming pool. After a minute, a tiny bird sitting on top of a trellis caught my attention. It was brown and yellow, like the bird that had fallen from the sky that day way back in Magborou.

"What should I do?" I asked the little weaver.

As the bird chirped three times and flew off, I remembered my flight after the rebel attack, my long walk alone in the bush, my close calls with barking dogs and spitting cobras. I saw the haggard face of the man who had led me to the clay road into Port Loko. I could still see his shaking hands as he passed me the mango to eat.

I knew then what I had to do. I may not have hands, but I have a voice. And no matter how nice my home in Canada is, my first home will always be Sierra Leone. The heart of my country is the heart of the people who helped me see myself not as a victim but as someone who could still do great things in this world.

I stood up, walked to my second-floor room, and opened my suitcase. I pulled out the formal red and gold Africana outfit that Kadi had made for me in Toronto. I smoothed out the creases and then pulled out of my travel bag a small box containing a pair of dangling gold earrings.

"Yes," I said out loud, even though the room was empty. "I

211

will meet the president tomorrow. I will speak for all the people of Sierra Leone who are not being heard."

Something in me had changed. I knew now that I could look forward *and* back—without any regrets—at the same time.

ШШ ΤΓΙ ШШ ΤΓΙ ШШ ΤΓΙ ШШ ΤΓΙ ШШ ΤΓΙ ШШ ΤΓΙ ШШ ΤΓΙ ШШ ΤΓΙ ШШ ΤΓΙ ШШ ΤΓΙ ШШ ΤΓΙ ШШ ΤΓΙ

To learn more about Mariatu and her current work in Sierra Leone, visit www.mariatufoundation.com.

ШШ ΤΓΙ ШШ ΤΓΙ ШШ ΤΓΙ ШШ ΤΓΙ ШШ ΤΓΙ ШШ ΤΓΙ ШШ ΤΓΙ ШШ ΤΓΙ ШШ ΤΓΙ ШШ ΤΓΙ ШШ ΤΓΙ ШШ ΤΓΙ

Sierra Leone

From 1991 to 2002, Sierra Leone was engaged in a brutal civil war. Armed rebels with the Revolutionary United Front (RUF) destroyed villages and farms, and raped, maimed, and murdered thousands of women and children.

Today, Sierra Leone, on the west coast of Africa, is one of the poorest countries in the world. In rural areas, the average wage is less than one dollar a day, life expectancy is only 40 years, and most children do not attend school on a regular basis.

Women and children have been hit especially hard by the war. Traditional village life, in which women were treated with respect by men, by their families, and by the larger community, no longer exists. Many women are subjected to ongoing sexual, emotional, and physical abuse, largely a result of the poverty brought on by large-scale unemployment. Men, unable to support their families from agriculture or other jobs, are alienated and angry. Children, particularly girls, often endure rape at the hands of older men, and are frequently forced into early marriages.

MARIATU KAMARA was born and raised in the West African nation of Sierra Leone. Her harrowing experiences as a child victim of war and the aftermath are the subject of her memoir, *The Bite of the Mango.*

Today, Mariatu is a college student in Toronto. She was named a UNICEF Special Representative for Children in Armed Conflicts, which involves speaking to groups across North America about her experiences. Prior to her UNICEF engagement, Mariatu spoke publicly for the nonprofit group, Free the Children.

Her professional goals for the future include working for the United Nations, raising awareness of the impact of war on children, and running her own foundation to raise money for a home, and eventually many homes, for abused women and children in Sierra Leone. She is also planning on reuniting several members of Aberdeen's theater troupe, which she credits with her personal healing. She would like to make this an ongoing project so that she can share with youth the peacekeeping skills that she is learning through her own work with UNICEF and others.

In her spare time, Mariatu likes to listen to music, cook, shop, talk on the phone, watch movies, and go to parties. Most of the time she likes to stay home with family and be with her close friends. She is torn between her love of Sierra Leone and Toronto. She wishes she could live in both places at the same time.

Photograph: Simon Tanenbaum

SUSAN MCCLELLAND is a freelance magazine journalist based in Toronto. Her work has appeared in *Macleans*, where she was a former staff writer, *Reader's Digest, More, Chatelaine, Canadian Living, The Walrus, Today's Parent,* and *The Globe and Mail.* She has won and been nominated for numerous investigative reporting and feature-writing awards, including National Magazine and Canadian Association of Journalists awards. Susan writes predominately on women's and children's issues and is the recipient of the 2005 Amnesty International Media Award. Her full biography and some of her articles can be viewed at **www.susanmcclelland.com**.